PRAISE FOR *Unique*

Being an effective communicator of your message is *biblical*. After all, Jesus didn't come across as out-of-touch and old-fashioned, so why should we? My advice? Read this book and let the superbly capable Phil Cooke carry you into your future.

Eric Metaxas, *New York Times* Bestselling Author, *Bonhoeffer: Pastor, Martyr, Prophet, Spy* and *Amazing Grace: William Wilberforce and the Heroic Campaign to End Slavery*

Phil Cooke is a media expert with unparalleled experience. *Unique* is a must-have for anyone serious about turning his or her story into a social media and branding blockbuster.

DeVon Franklin, Vice President of Production, Columbia Pictures

Without a doubt, Phil Cooke is a genius. If you want your story to be heard amongst the thousands of conflicting and competing messages out there, *Unique* is the book for you. Full of great practical advice, humor and common sense, you will find yourself referring to this book often!

Christine Caine, Founder, The A21 Campaign

What is a brand? What is your brand? Why should anyone care? If you can't answer these questions, read Phil's book!

Jesse Bryan, Creative Director, Mars Hill Church

Within a 24/7 riptide of new technologies and communication resources, it's sink or surge. *Unique* comes at just the right time with practical and timely tools for today's leaders to rise to thrilling new mission impact.

Geof Morin, Chief Communications Officer, American Bible Society

One of the best things a church can do is stop and think about how it is perceived by the world around it. My friend Phil Cooke understands the power of branding, which is why I am excited about this book! Read it, and you will never again look at church identity the same way.

Greg Surratt, Senior Pastor, Seacoast Church
Author, *Ir-Rev-Rend*

Phil's book is smart, original, practical and comprehensive. It's completely relevant to any person of faith living in today's culture who wants to undo some of the unintended damage Christians have done. Gain some ground and read this. It's honest, objective, empowering and on my top ten must-read book list.

Kem Meyer, Communications Director, Granger Community Church

Unique should be read twice by everyone who wants to communicate his or her life message in a compelling way. Phil's ideas are challenging, and his message is inspiring. Take this unique opportunity to let Phil be your coach and your friend.

Philip Wagner, Lead Pastor of Oasis Church, Los Angeles
Author, *How to Turn Your Marriage Around in 10 Days*

Of the many successful organizations and leaders I know, they have two things in common: (1) they have little in common, and (2) they have Phil Cooke's influence on their brand. Phil's fusion of skepticism, sincerity, salesmanship and, at times, scathing brilliancy will make you savvy "Wall Street" smart! Phil's writing will cause you to question why you do what you do without losing your quest to keep doing it—better! You are about to discern and discover a brand new you!

Phil Munsey, Pastor, Life Church, Irvine, California
Chairman, Joel Osteen's Champions Network

Everyone wants to stand out in today's crowded marketplace, but few do. Phil Cooke always has. In *Unique,* he personally guides you on an insightful journey into sharing your story in today's culture, giving you practical guidance on navigating the opportunities social media provides. Loaded with stories and simple tips, Phil has provided a compelling charge to take your brand seriously.

Rob Hoskins, President, One Hope

Phil Cooke has always had an amazing way of helping people enlarge their lives using his practical tips. Captured in the pages of this book are nuggets of wisdom that will help you take the thing about you that is truly " unique" and make it stand out in a very crowded world.

Ron Carpenter Jr., Pastor, Redemption World Outreach Center

In *Unique*, Phil Cooke takes us beyond lamenting the ill effects of our media-driven culture to thinking about how to effectively present who we are—and who Jesus is—through new forms such as branding, design and social media. But Phil also powerfully reminds us that we must have something worth communicating. He challenges us to honestly understand who we are and shows us how to be authentic and transparent. Jesus told us to be "in the world" but not "of the world" (see John 15:19). Phil tells us how to do that today!

Erick Schenkel, Executive Director, The *JESUS* Film Project

Unique is a must-read if you want your product or organization to find relevancy in an increasingly complicated world. As Phil points out, "Branding is simply the art of surrounding a product, organization, or person with a powerful and compelling story." This new book can help you or your organization break through to become a compelling story.

Frank S. Page, President and CEO, Executive Committee
of the Southern Baptist Convention

Unique is a must-read for any church or nonprofit organization looking to increase their influence and get their message out to the masses. *Unique* is full of practical steps to effectively sharpen your core message and use technology to rapidly spread it. Don't miss this opportunity to grow your ministry or nonprofit—get this book!

Bil Cornelius, Lead Pastor, Bay Area Fellowship
Author, *I Dare You to Change*

Unique is another one of Phil Cooke's innovative resources. This book is a literary tutor that will show you how to wrap your story with a strategic brand and leverage all media to get that story told!

Charles Jenkins, Pastor, Fellowship Missionary Baptist Church, Chicago, Illinois

Phil Cooke makes me think and be thankful. He makes me think because he's always challenging me to be more effective in all things media, and he makes me thankful because he is helping the twenty-first century Church carry out the Great Commission in a much greater manner. He is the leading voice in all things media. I recommend Phil Cooke to churches regularly.

Dr. Samuel R. Chand, Author, *Cracking Your Church's Culture Code*

As Phil says in *Unique,* like it or not we all make some kind of impact on people, and because we will make an impact, we had better figure out how to manage our brand so others don't manage it for us in a negative way. *Unique* shows us how to cut through all the noise, use media effectively, and ensure that our message is heard. Phil Cooke is an authority on media and ministry branding, and this book provides the tools that can help us get results beyond our wildest dreams.

Dr. Arnie Cole, CEO, Back to the Bible
Author, *Unstuck*

For most of us who live in the day-to-day grind of branding and marketing, Phil Cooke is the whisperer—the guy who is asking the hard questions. *Unique* will soon become required reading for anyone who wants to carve out his or her space in today's crowded markets. No one understands new media and the all-important "finding your voice" like Phil. I am honored to endorse this book and, more importantly, Phil Cooke.

Timothy Smith, Chief Development Officer, Food for the Hungry

Phil has a unique ability to communicate to all generations of leaders in a way that is humorous, practical and understandable. *Unique* will inspire you and equip you with the tools to find your voice and identity in a world that is constantly changing. I highly recommend this book to those who are looking to get their message out to the world.

Jordan Wagner, Executive Director, GenerosityWater.com

Your brand comprises the perceptions you own and the promises you make. So, how is it going? Are the perceptions and promises in your brand helping or hurting? Is your brand a powerful engine supporting your mission, or is it a heavy sea anchor hindering your progress? To find that answer and get the valuable help you need in crafting a compelling brand, I highly recommend *Unique.* It may be one of the most important books you read all year.

Frank Wright, Ph.D., President and CEO
National Religious Broadcasters (NRB)

As anyone involved in communicating Christian truth knows, the world is changing at a speed that threatens to leave us behind. This insightful, timely and provocative book is a challenging guide on how to say what we ought to say in our new media-driven culture. If you want your message to be heard in the age of Facebook and Twitter, you need to read this book.

Rev. Canon J. John, Speaker and Author

We all wish for more hours in a day, but we can actually have more focus, produce more results, and tell our story with more impact through this amazing book. Stop looking through the quotes and buy *Unique* now. Phil is an absolute genius.

Pastor David McGee, Pastor, The Bridge Church
Host, "Cross the Bridge" Media Ministries

I have known Phil Cooke for just a few years, but I have consistently been struck by his unique perspective and insight. There is just something about him that is relevant and refreshing. In *Unique,* with simplicity and clarity, he exorcises your fears of branding and helps you tell the story of your faith and ministry. You will become comfortable with how branding can serve a ministry, learn how to identify your specific brand, and, through the process, become *brand* new. Use *Unique* as a textbook. The result will be an increase in impact for the kingdom of God.

Bishop Kyle Searcy, Pastor, Fresh Anointing House of Worship, Montgomery, Alabama
Apostolic Council, International Communion of Evangelical Churches (ICEC)

Unique

Telling Your Story
in the Age of Brands
and Social Media

PHIL COOKE

Regal

For more information and
special offers from Regal Books, email us at
subscribe@regalbooks.com

Published by Regal
From Gospel Light
Ventura, California, U.S.A.
www.regalbooks.com
Printed in the U.S.A.

Revised and updated from *Branding Faith,* originally published
by Regal Books in 2008.

Library of Congress Cataloging-in-Publication Data
Cooke, Phil, 1954-
Unique : telling your story in the age of brands and social media / Phil Cooke.
p. cm.
Includes bibliographical references and index.
ISBN 978-0-8307-6515-7 (trade paper : alk. paper)
1. Christianity and culture. 2. Christianity—Influence. 3. Social media.
4. Branding (Marketing) 5. Storytelling—Religious aspects—Christianity.
I. Title.
BR115.C8C596 2012
261–dc23
2012023489

Rights for publishing this book outside the U.S.A. or in non-English
languages are administered by Gospel Light Worldwide, an international
not-for-profit ministry. For additional information, please visit
www.glww.org, email info@glww.org, or write to Gospel Light Worldwide,
1957 Eastman Avenue, Ventura, CA 93003, U.S.A.

To order copies of this book and other Regal products in bulk quantities,
please contact us at 1-800-446-7735.

Contents

ACKNOWLEDGMENTS

I've said many times that I don't write books because I have all the answers; I write because I have lots of questions. Those questions have been answered time and time again, over a long career and with the help of a number of wonderful clients who allowed me the creative space to experiment, learn and grow. To all our faith-based and nonprofit clients, I'm grateful for your encouragement and inspiration over the years.

I also want to thank my incredible team at Cooke Pictures who have provided the support, motivation and ideas that have made a dramatic difference for our clients.

My agent Rachelle Gardner encouraged me to update my original manuscript to reflect the constantly changing world of technology and communications.

Daniel Long was instrumental in helping me research and write additional information about the ever-changing world of social media.

Stan Jantz, Kim Bangs, and the team at Regal have been incredibly supportive in helping connect this book to a new generation of communicators.

Finally, I'm grateful to my brilliant wife, Kathleen, and daughters, Kelsey and Bailey, and sons-in law, Chris and Jeremy, who have allowed me the freedom to travel in pursuit of this information, and more important, given me a fantastic reason to come back home.

Phil Cooke
July 15, 2012

In 2007, when I completed the manuscript of my book *Branding Faith*, the world was a different place. Before the advent of the twenty-first century, that kind of statement was only made regarding generational change, and even that was rare. Prior to 1900, measuring global change happened in 1- to 500-year increments. But in the five years between *Branding Faith*'s first appearance on the bookshelves and the date of this printing, the world indeed has become a dramatically different place.

The Social Media Explosion

First, in 2007, social media had not yet taken the world by storm. There were many early social media applications, but most people entered the social media swimming pool through MySpace, then went into the deep end with Facebook. Founded officially in 2004 as "The Facebook" (thefacebook.com), it lingered largely as a tool for finding friends in college—perhaps more accurately, for finding *girls* in college. It began at Harvard and moved out from there. At the time, I remember my 20-something assistant scrambling to see if her college email address was still active so she could join, since it only allowed college students to be members.

The rest, as they say, is history. By December 2011, Facebook's own statistics reveal it had more than 600 million members, by population making it the third largest country in the world, just behind China and India.

Twitter began in 2006, and after a year or so began to experience similar explosive growth. As of 2011, it had expanded to 300 million members; and by the time you read this, it will have grown to considerably more.

In both cases (and other social media like LinkedIn, Google+, Pinterest, Tagged, and many others), what began as a novelty has become a powerful global tool for influence and connectivity. Twitter was a key player in the 2011 Egyptian revolution, the 2010–2011 Tunisian protests, the 2009 Iranian election protests, and city unrest throughout Eastern Europe. It's been used by presidents and politicians, as well as rock stars and celebrities. It was enormously helpful in getting the word out about the Haiti earthquake, the tsunami in Japan and other crisis hot zones.

So, my first desire in writing this book was to pick up where *Branding Faith* left off and address social media and how it impacts your brand. In 2007, social media wasn't even on the radar for many organizations in America; but today, major companies and nonprofits wouldn't consider a communications strategy without including it.

The *Branding Faith* Revolution

Second, when *Branding Faith* was originally published, the vast majority of leaders in the church, ministry and nonprofit world still thought a "brand" was something burned into a cow's hide. Certainly they understood the power of a compelling brand in terms of *secular* companies and businesses. But to bring that thinking into the religious world was almost sacrilege.

It just wasn't done.

So the book encountered a wall of opposition from some sectors of the church. After all, it was the first book to actually deal with the religious implications on a major level, so it took some time to change people's thinking. But gradually the light started switching on and momentum picked up. One major ministry leader ordered 77 copies of the book—one for each board member and department head in the organization. Others bought multiple copies for the leadership team or pastoral staff. Many major demoninations and church networks asked me to speak or asked for advice on how to shape their own perceptions and brand.

In fact, since the publication date, numerous "branding agencies" have popped up across the country specifically to help churches, ministries and nonprofit organzations define their own brand strategy. Some have done very well, but others are giving some bad advice, and I want to address some of that branding "heresy" floating around.

What About Your Personal Brand?

Finally, I updated my original book to address the importance of how a compelling brand impacts a *person*. Before the publication of *Branding Faith,* I had spent my career helping major religious and nonprofit organizations engage the culture more effectively. Our team's work was about helping large churches, ministries and nonprofits define their story and share it with the world. But after releasing the book, I realized just how much these branding principles can define your *individual* story as well.

I started receiving emails from writers, filmmakers, entrepreneurs, artists, pastors and others about how they were using the book to define how they connect with audiences, investors, studios and donors to get their ideas heard. So I've changed my approach just enough to show you how to apply these overarching principles that have changed *organizations* to changing your *career*. Whether you're a pastor or ministry leader, business leader, filmmaker, writer, artist, muscian or anyone else with an idea or message to share, these important principles will make just as much impact helping you cut through today's distracted culture and get on the radar.

   Much of the original book is still here, and it's good to rethink those ideas. But even if you have read the original *Branding Faith*, I would encourage you to take this new and improved journey once again. It will open your eyes to new possibilities and help you understand how today's social media platforms will make a difference in sharing your message with the world.

Responding to a Media-driven Culture

> Men of Issachar, who understood the times and knew what Israel should do.
>
> 1 Chronicles 12:32

> O ye hypocrites, ye can discern the face of the sky; but can ye not discern the signs of the times?
>
> Matthew 16:3, *KJV*

My wife, Kathleen, and I were enjoying a relaxing weekend retreat with some friends in the entertainment industry when someone asked an intriguing question: Why do so many Christians do such a terrible job of presenting their message to the world?

As a producer and director in the industry, who also works as a consultant and writer on issues of media and faith, I encounter that question on a fairly frequent basis. In a country where pastors used to be high on the credibility scale, today it seems as if they've fallen nearly to the level of con artists. If you've read David Kinnaman and Gabe Lyon's fascinating book, *unChristian: What a New Generation Really Thinks About Christianity . . . and Why It Matters,* which features extensive research about what the greater culture thinks about Christians, then you will know what I mean.

This generation has grown up watching endless fights about religion and politics, culture bashing and a host of other ideological battles; and most are, frankly, tired of the brawl. Across the spectrum, organized religious faith has taken a beating in the public square. As a result, how unbelievers perceive the Christian community could use a little help.

I answered my friend's question by sharing a passionate belief that in a media-driven culture, we need to do a better job of telling our story. In essence, we need to understand the power of branding and identity, and seriously reconsider how we express our faith to a skeptical and unbelieving world.

One member of the group that weekend, a brilliant writer and producer of big-budget comedy movies, who is also a very serious believer, began to turn pale. He turned to me (almost in disgust) and said, "I don't think you could have said anything that would have hurt me more. The idea that we should reduce Christianity to a 'brand' is completely offensive."

A similar event happened a few weeks later, when an online blogger found an advertisement for a lecture I was giving on branding Christian organizations. He posted the ad on his website and proceeded to rip apart the concept that someone could "brand the Christian faith." He thought it was cheap and sleazy to even consider such an insulting idea.

After those two events, both of which were driven by well-meaning people, I realized I had a branding problem of my own.

In today's world, the concept of branding carries a lot of negative baggage. As I'll point out later in this book, many people associate branding with much of the criticism and condemnation they hear about the "evils" of corporate America. From environmental destruction, rampant consumerism, globalism, destruction of local cultures, rising personal debt and more, the word "branding" has become an ugly catchall term that covers just about anything distasteful or extreme about big business.

The Wall Street crisis of 2008 didn't help. Suddenly, anything that smacked of capitalism didn't seem appropriate for the church. But the truth is, branding isn't about crass commercialism, manipulation, corporate abuses or bad advertising. The AIGA Center for Brand Experience calls it simply, "A person's perception of a product, service, experience, or organization." I prefer to call it "the *story* that surrounds a product, service, person or organization." In other words:

What do people think of when they think of you, your product or your organization?

As I'll explain in much greater detail later in the book, the issue is ultimately about *perception*—how your customer, audience, donor, supporter or even church member perceives his or her experience with your organization. For much of this book, we'll focus on how people perceive their encounters with a local church; a ministry; a religious media program; a nonprofit and humanitarian organization, college or university; or any other religious or nonprofit outreach, including the products and experiences they create.

But we won't stop there. After all, Oprah, LA Laker Kobe Bryant, Joel Osteen, the host of *NBC News*, the Pope, your pastor, your doctor and the Super Bowl MVP all have a brand, and *you* have a brand. *What do people think of when they think of you* isn't just about organizations; it's about *people* as well.

You may want to pitch a book idea, a film treatment, a new business, a website, a sermon series, song or something else. But whatever it is, if that executive, donor, investor, customer or audience doesn't have an immediate, positive impression of you, you can kiss your dream goodbye.

To attempt to "re-brand" the Christian faith itself would be absurd. As James Twitchell states in his book *Branded Nation,* God is a *belief*, not a *brand*.[1] The Christian faith in particular has done very well on its own for the last 2,000-plus years. It has literally transformed the West and created orphanages, hospitals, universities and countless humanitarian outreaches. Biblical references fill the pages of our greatest books. Music, art and literature would be poor indeed without its remarkable influence. Argue all you want about the belief itself, but there's no question that Christianity has been a powerful force that has changed the world for the better.

However, at this particular moment in history, I propose that we need to dramatically change the way we publicly *express* that belief. A critical key to accomplishing that goal is understanding how we are perceived—or *branded*.

If you're a follower of Jesus, your vocation is your story. That's your business and calling. Jesus-followers are in the story business.

Leonard Sweet
Writer and Social Critic

Throughout the history of the Church, leaders and communicators of the faith have struggled against the various cultures in which they have found themselves. During the dangerous days of the Early Church, the apostles lived and worked against the backdrop of the Roman occupation of the Middle East. Others since then have struggled against cultures of discrimination, hostility and outright violence; and even today, many Christians in different countries continue to express their faith under the looming threat of arrest and execution.

During some centuries, the Christian faith was virtually a *civil* religion. We now look back at what we call Christendom—when Christianity was as much a social and political force as a religious issue. By contrast, my father was a pastor during the 1950s and '60s when the debate wasn't about the *influence* of God but about the "death" of God. In every case, just as Paul did in the New Testament, as recorded in Acts 17, anyone who attempted to present the Christian message in a relevant way knew they had to recognize and understand the cultural framework of the time in order to be an effective communicator.

Media Is Culture

Today, the Church in the West struggles under a different framework: *the power of global media*. As I'll show later in this book, the media's influence in our lives is pervasive. Education, business, religion, leisure and even family life are all measured against that influence. And when it comes to media, we live in the most hyper-competitive, distracted and disrupted culture in history.

The answer to "Who's influencing the Church today?" is the same as "Who's influencing the culture?"

It's the media.

That's why our challenge today is how to express our faith in a media-dominated world. How do we tell our story alongside the maddening swirl of TV, radio, computer, mobile, Internet, social media and other technologies competing for our attention? Throughout the book, I'll call these things "clutter."

How do we get our message heard through the massive and growing amount of media static out there?

Stay tuned.

> What does religion look like from a marketing point of view? Mind you, I'm not talking about God. That's a belief, not a brand. A brand is a story that travels with a product or service or, in this case, a concept. In the beginning of Christianity was the Word, and, as I'm sure you've already guessed, the Word was the Brand.
>
> **James B. Twitchell**
> Branded Nation[1]

Losing Our Voice

My team gets hired when a church, ministry or nonprofit organization has lost its voice.

Perhaps you've experienced a similar situation: In spite of doing great works in the community, like building homeless shelters, drug treatment centers or food banks, your organization still lives hand to mouth. Or, as a pastor or religious leader who has had a genuine calling, you have built a great team, invested your life in the vision with powerful preaching, teaching or ministry, but the spark never happens; growth never takes off or it just suddenly stops.

After years or decades of work, nobody seems to care. No one seems to be listening, even though your book idea, movie, or dream project has such enormous possibilities. You really believe that if they will just *listen*, it can change their lives. But for whatever reason, you've lost your impact and lost your voice to the very people with whom you're trying to communicate.

I see it happen all too often: Media ministries that just can't seem to grow beyond a local broadcast; churches that hit a ceiling on adding members; humanitarian outreaches that can't seem to break through a certain level of fund-raising. In most cases, they are led by qualified, sincere men and women, and almost all have a strong vision for excellence. They spend money on capital campaigns; media equipment; church-growth consultants; marketing, TV or radio time; advertising and social media campaigns, and more, but they just seem trapped and unable to grow beyond a certain point.

They're just not getting their message across.

A number of years ago, I was invited to the monthly creative and marketing meeting for one of the largest Christian media ministries in the world. The media-buying company had actually asked me to come because, for some time, they had noticed that the television viewers—although historically a large audience—had stopped growing. Once they began investigating, they discovered it was pretty much the same story throughout the entire ministry. Income had hit a plateau, product sales were flat, TV response was slowing and financial partnership with donors was almost nonexistent.

When I was introduced to the ministry leader—a prominent religious leader—his first response was, "Well, I don't know why you're here. There's nothing wrong with *this* organization."

The media buyer tried to explain that because of my work with a number of the largest nonprofit organizations in the country, I might offer them some advice on how to break through the ceiling that was holding them back.

His response was blunt. "I watch lots of religious television, and our program is as good as anything I see out there. I don't know how you could possibly help us."

The room got a bit icy, and it felt like the temperature was dropping quickly.

I stood up and walked around the room. In a respectful tone, I replied, "I think you're absolutely correct. Your program is well produced and your ministry has always been very popular. But the truth is, you've suddenly hit a wall that no one seems to be able to explain." (His program did have some issues, but nothing insurmountable.)

I continued, "Before I came to this meeting, I spent time studying the different expressions of the ministry, and the first thing I noticed was that everything you do looks different from everything else."

I pulled out pictures from the ministry website, the title card from the opening of the television program, the website design, some recent DVD product sets, a print ad, a brochure and his latest book. I pointed out that they all looked like they came from five or six different organizations. There was no common look or theme to anything—they all appeared to be designed by six different artists. Essentially, they were telling six different (and sometimes conflicting) stories about the ministry.

The Power of Unifying the Story

When you look at the advertising from a major brand like Nike, Starbucks or Apple Computer, everything they do—from bus stop ads to television to magazines—has a common look and style. From a hundred yards away you can recognize a McDonald's restaurant. It doesn't matter if you're in Beijing, Mumbai, Cleveland or Moscow. Its recognizibility is one of its great strengths. These companies all carry the theme of the business across all media, which in turn strengthens the power of the company in the minds of the consumer.

I got his attention.

"So how do we fix that?" he asked.

"Tell me who you are," I replied.

"We're a teaching ministry that's called to preach and teach the message of Jesus Christ."

I urged him to be more specific, saying, "That's no different from a million other churches and ministries out there."

"Okay, we're called to television."

"Still no good." I decided to push him a bit. "The question isn't, What do you do? or, How do you do it? The real question here is, Who *are* you?" He stopped for a second, and I said:

> ### "Let me put it this way: What do people think of when they think of you?"

He had no answer. He'd never thought of it before.

Look around the religious media landscape in this country. The National Religious Broadcasters—the professional association for religious media ministries—boasts more than 1,400 member organizations. But that's a drop in the bucket compared to the hundreds of thousands of churches and ministries across the country and around the globe.

It's no different in the nonprofit world. Museums, homeless shelters, after-school programs, universities and more are all driven by the ability to raise funding. But how do you stand out in your community?

The problem is not just about particularly large organizations. In fact, it's often especially critical in local neighborhood churches or small nonprofits.

And sometimes, it's just about you and your personal dream.

In a world of wide-ranging choices, people need categories. In an age of skepticism and media diversification, they need to easily understand who you are and how to relate to your idea or dream. Otherwise, you'll be lost in the sea of alternatives.

The Competition Is Greater than Ever

Want to publish a book? In 2011, 300,000 books were published by traditional publishers, and that doesn't count the additional 3 million that were self-published.

How about producing a feature film? During the same period, 1,000 movies were released in the United States.

Maybe you could start with a YouTube video? According to their own statistics, 60 hours of video are uploaded to YouTube every *minute*.

Television isn't any better. The average cable TV system in America now has 160 channels, with some satelite systems boasting as many as 500 channels.

What about a great business idea? The U.S. government's own statistics reveal that in spite of today's tough economy, 500,000 businesses were opened in 2011, all competing for the same investor money.

Okay, so how about a nonprofit? In 2011 alone, 1.6 million nonprofits were registered with the IRS.

Whatever good this abundance brings to the world, it also brings confusion and clutter for people who are trying to make sense of it all. The ministry leader I was meeting with began to understand. "So how do audiences relate to people and ministries they see out there right now?" he asked.

I encouraged him to consider radio and TV ministries during the last 20 years or so. The most successful ministries may teach on a wide variety of issues, but in most cases, they each have an overarching theme to their life and ministry. Until he retired from pastoral ministry a few years ago, my own pastor was Jack Hayford at The Church On The Way, in Van Nuys, California. As a pastor, Jack was a brilliant teacher and spent decades preaching and teaching on an incredibly wide range of subjects in response to God's calling and the needs of the congregation. But in spite of that range and depth, I believe that Jack was and is motivated and driven by worship. He is endlessly fascinated with the subject, both as a pastor and as a musician. As a result, he has taught today's Church volumes on the issue. Many would say he's the single greatest voice in the Christian community on the importance of godly worship in the church today.

Bottom line, if you cut Jack, he bleeds worship.

I rattled off a list of other names from the world of media ministry, both past and present. Whether you agree with their theology or not, here's who they are in most people's minds:

- Billy Graham is the *salvation* guy.
- Kenneth Copeland is the *faith* guy.
- Rick Warren is the *purpose* guy.
- John Maxwell is the *leadership* guy.
- Rod Parsley is the *Pentecostal* guy.
- James Dobson is the *family* guy.
- Joel Osteen is the *inspirational* guy.
- Dave Ramsey is the *financial* guy.
- Joyce Meyer is about *enjoying everyday life.*

Granted, you may consider this a crude way to look at it, but for millions of people, that's exactly how they view these ministry personalities. In a world of choices, defining these ministries gives the audience an easy handle and allows them to have a quick understanding of who a particular pastor or ministry leader is and where his or her focus lies. Why is this necessary? Think of your brain as acting like a filter to help you sort through the growing flood of information that surrounds you every day.

Branding consultant Marty Neumeier calls today's culture *information-rich and time-poor.* In this environment, we need easy ways to help us get to the real information we need to make decisions about life.

To the viewer, supporter or church member, it's ultimately about a person, church or organization's identity—helping people understand who they are and what they mean to a person's life.

It's about the story that surrounds who you are— a story that creates focus for your ministry.

In short, it's about your brand.

I ask you the same thing I asked that ministry leader in our creative meeting: *What do people think of when they think of you?*

A successful church, ministry or nonprofit organization happens at the intersection of a number of issues, not the least of which is calling, vision, ability, commitment, resources, exposure, location and education. There's no question that a pastor who can't preach will face obstacles; an evangelist with no calling will eventually collapse; and the leader of any nonprofit organization with no vision will never get very far.

This book, however, is about what happens when all those things fall into place and the spark *still* doesn't happen: when a church with all the right ingredients still struggles; when a gifted pastor never reaches a larger audience; when a wonderful ministry can't seem to break through a particular barrier; or when your great idea just isn't getting through to the right people.

It could also happen to a church or ministry of any size that has been successful in the past, but like the pastor in my creative meeting, suddenly and with no explanation, the ministry stops getting results.

> When that happens, it's not about what you do;
> it's about how you're perceived.

In a media-driven culture, when even the best idea doesn't have a clear and compelling story surrounding it, no amount of qualifications, resources, advertising or leadership can overcome the deficit. And it doesn't even matter if the organization or person has experienced great success in the past. As James Twitchell, in his book *Branded Nation*, reminds us, "Observe the current state of the once-dominant Episcopal Church. Episcopalians committed an unforgivable marketing sin: they forgot their brand because they lost their story."[2]

Ideas Are Powerful, and Stories Are Ideas in Action

I hosted a 10-year anniversary event for a European nonprofit satellite TV network. The formal event was held in the Ronald Reagan Presidential Library in Simi Valley, California. Before the dinner, we were taken on a tour of the presidential museum, of Ronald and

Nancy's private quarters and even were given a tour of Air Force One, majestically enshrined in its own wing of the museum.

> I did everything they told me in seminary. I was a good preacher, had a committed ministry team, hired the right church-growth experts and fundraisers; I prayed until my carpet wore through and still never went beyond a local ministry. Was that God's plan for me? Possibly; but I couldn't help but wonder how the new media world has impacted our outreach, and if I was missing that connection.
>
> **Pastor in the Midwest**

As we walked through the exhibits—particularly the areas chronicling President Reagan's role in the fall of the Soviet Union—I was captivated by a powerful inscription on the wall of the exhibit. It was a quote from Soviet leader Joseph Stalin:

Ideas are more powerful than guns. We would not let our enemies have guns, why should we let them have ideas?

The quotation stands in clear testimony to the power of ideas and just how desperately the Soviet Union attempted to control those ideas. Today, that scenario is being played out as the government of Iran desperately studies how China has grown their economy while still controlling the political ideas of its population. In fact, in 2012, the Chinese Communist Party reaffirmed their ban on religion for all members. They want the booming economy that innovation brings while, at the same time, controlling the ideas that make innovation happen.

Just like the former Soviet Union, and now China, the leadership of Iran understands the explosive power of ideas.

This book isn't about public relations; it's about ideas. It's about using the power of storytelling to create a life-changing impression of you and your organization in the minds of your viewers, church members, partners, visitors and supporters. It's not about manipulation, but about helping people clearly understand who you are and how you can impact their lives.

The media today is a digital cacophony of voices and images. To stand out in that ocean of choices takes more than excellent sermons, quality resources, professional programs and good intentions.

Connecting with a Culture that Changes at Light Speed

Shortly after the invasion of Afghanistan, I watched a national television news program broadcast a "discussion" (read: debate) about America's decision to invade that country in pursuit of terrorism. The discussion focused on religious leaders from various backgrounds, and it had the usual cast of characters:

- A successful New Age religious writer
- A liberal bishop from a major denomination
- A popular teacher of Eastern religion
- A well-known conservative pastor and radio preacher

As I listened to the interview, I first paid attention to the integrity of their arguments. The first three offered glib sound-bite responses to the questions. These particular men were intellectually shallow, and it didn't take long to see that they didn't have any real answers. Apparently, they had been chosen because of their media popularity rather than their academic or political insight. But when it came to their attitude and demeanor, I noticed they were warm and friendly. They looked the interviewer directly in the eye and were engaging and conversational.

The conservative pastor and radio preacher was actually far more eloquent and solid in his answers. He had a strong biblical response and was intellectually deep, and his words made real sense. On the other hand, he was cold and unfriendly—almost arrogant. He refused to engage the others and instead appeared aloof and condescending.

At the end, I realized that although the conservative pastor had presented far better and more authoritative answers, in the eye of the viewers he had lost the debate. I felt so frustrated at the disconnect between his abilities and people's perception of him that I wrote him a letter. To my surprise, he wrote back.

His answer was essentially: "I don't care. God didn't call me to be liked. After all, they liked Jesus, and they crucified Him. I'm called to speak the truth, and frankly, I don't care what people think."

An earlier generation might have interpreted that response as bold and uncompromising. But I interpret it as being ignorant of the times in which we live.

When you persuade, speak of interest, not of reason.
Benjamin Franklin

That pastor clearly didn't have a clue about how to communicate in a media-driven culture. I would never question his answers in the discussion or even the intent of his heart, but I would argue with how his supercilious and arrogant attitude turned away many who might have been impacted by his remarks. People establish a gut-level connection with a person based on their own values and perceptions long before they buy into the person's message.

Admit it—when you meet a person for the first time, you've sized him (or her) up long before he opens his mouth. You perceive through the person's attitude, clothes, weight, the watch on his arm or the car he drives. Sure, it may not be right, but we naturally do it all the time.

That's what political consultants and writers Douglas B. Sosnick, Matthew J. Dowd and Ron Fournier discovered in the book *Applebee's America: How Successful Political, Business, and Religious Leaders Connect with the New American Culture*:

> Values are what Americans want to see in a candidate, corporation, or church before they're even willing to consider their policies and products. The choices people make about politics, consumer goods, and even religion are driven by emotions, rather than intellect.[3]

That's not a criticism of intellectual pursuit; and I wish more churches in America taught deeper doctrinal principles. But when a consumer makes the initial connection, it's not about *content*; it's about the *brand*. The values, story and sense of authenticity that surround a political candidate, business person, filmmaker or religious leader are far more important in that first moment.

There was a time when "packaging" had little impact on ministry, but not today. For a visually oriented, media-savvy generation, it's about more than just the message; it's also about the medium. And it's about the *brand*.

A Media-driven Culture Changes the Equation for Ministry

The apostle Paul lived out his ministry in the context of Roman domination; William Wilberforce campaigned in Parliament under the shadow of the British slave trade; Dietrich Bonhoeffer struggled under Nazi occupation. Today, we live in a media-dominated culture and must operate our churches, ministries or nonprofit organizations in that technological context.

Unique

In a previous age, all a preacher needed to be successful was a good Bible, a calling from God and strong lungs. But in today's digital culture, where a typical American deals with as many as 5,000 media messages a day, how does the voice of your church, ministry, nonprofit organization or idea rise above the racket?

Living in a Media-driven Culture

> Entertainment—not autos,
> not steel, not financial services—
> is fast becoming the driving wheel
> of the new world economy.
>
> **Michael J. Wolf**
> *The Entertainment Economy*[1]

I once heard it said that if an alien from another planet were to examine the United States and write an evaluation of our religious habits, he would probably conclude that Oprah is America's pastor; the vestments of the twenty-first-century church are manufactured by Nike; the Communion table is poured by a barista from Starbucks; and in the children's department, a clown from McDonald's is certainly more widely recognized than Jesus of Nazareth. Today, people confess their sins on daytime television, purge their guilt by donating to TV evangelists, and seek redemption through the story arc in an action movie.

This information isn't anything new. At a typical religious conference today, people will debate the collapse of moral values; discuss the impact of living in an entertainment culture; or argue whether or not we should protest, boycott or engage.

Many blame growing polarization in politics on the widening gap between the church and state; others point to the growing permissiveness of society; and still others fault explicit sex and violence in the media. No matter how you look at it, culture today is far more coarse, ragged and uncertain than it was a generation ago.

As people have done since the beginning of time, when society feels uncertain, they look for spiritual answers. Religious belief comforts us during times of difficulty. It provides a moral bearing and imparts meaning and purpose that materialism simply can't provide.

During the last few years, there has been a trend in advertising and marketing to explore the connections between religion and branding. As advertisers search for more and more effective ways to connect products with consumers, they've stumbled upon the power of "meaning." If you can link a product to a consumer's personal identity, the connection becomes far stronger and the relationship sticks for a much longer period of time.

That's no surprise to the Church, which has known its impact for thousands of years. The Bible itself says, "Train up a child in the way he should go, and when he is old he will not depart from it" (Prov. 22:6, *NKJV*). As a preacher's kid growing up in the South, I heard my father preach that if you could get young people into church as children, the chances were far higher that they would continue that relationship for the rest of their lives.

Today, mobile phone companies, fashion designers, food producers, television networks, and more, focus specifically on children in order to make them brand conscious for life.

A Brand Stays Forever

Branding is about identity. Even in the nuclear age, there isn't a more powerful force on the earth. "Identity politics" is changing the political scene as gays, feminists and ethnic groups all want a place at the table. Wars are fought over cultural identity, and seemingly normal people commit horrific crimes simply to save face. Here in Los Angeles, gang members are willing to die for other members, even though they barely know them. Gang identity on the streets is so strong that few things—sometimes not even family ties—can break that hold.

Who we are is an issue of identity, integrity and purpose, and we're willing to go to great lengths to keep that identity unique and strong.

The faster globalism removes barriers,
the faster people erect new ones.
They create intimate worlds they can
understand, and where they can be
somebody and feel as if they belong.
They create tribes.

Marty Neumeier
The Brand Gap[2]

It's natural that marketers should look to religion for inspiration. Religion is all about identity. *Who am I? Why am I here? What's my purpose in life?* I believe in it so much that I wrote the book *One Big Thing: Discovering What You Were Born to Do.* The focus of the book is to help people understand how to tap into the overarching purpose for their lives. I believe it's one of the most important questions we can ask.

In future chapters, we'll discuss many of the current thinkers who have made the connection between branding and religion; but for the most part, they are looking from the outside in. For my purposes, I'm more interested in examining the question from the opposite direction. As I said, I'm a preacher's kid who grew up in the church during turbulent times in its history. During the fifties and sixties, the church was struggling for its identity amid the "death of God" theologians, the creeping liberalism of the Church and the ongoing culture wars. During that time, the Church changed dramatically as evangelicalism grew, charismatic and Pentecostal churches exploded, and we experienced a major shift in church growth. Historic mainline denominations took sides on the issue of the "social gospel," and pastors debated the role of the supernatural and the legitimacy of Christ's miracles.

Out of that, a church emerged that was populated by a younger generation that understood the power of media, that was not content with what they perceived as propaganda, and that searched for new methods to share an eternal message.

Having experienced those changes on the front lines of ministry, I became one of the new breed of believers in America. Rather than pursue my father's calling as a pastor, I finished a bachelor's degree in television and film studies, a master's in journalism, and a Ph.D. in theology. It took awhile, but my goal was to merge the historic Christian faith with more effective methods of sharing that story in a media-driven culture. Since that time, I've produced programs in nearly 50 countries around the world, split my work between secular and religious programming, and consulted on media issues for some of the largest and most effective churches and nonprofit organizations in the world.

My goal was simple: How do we share a life-changing message with a culture that has lost interest? How can our message compete with the cacophony of voices in the media? How have churches and religious organizations become so irrelevant? Why is religious media so out of touch with the culture? If we are actually speaking Truth with a capital T, why isn't anyone listening?

As a result, it wasn't long before I realized that when it came to actually impacting the culture, the Church has a huge problem:

We've lost our story.

From the earliest days of Hebrew storytellers sitting around campfires in the deserts of the Middle East, storytelling has been the core of every culture known to man. From the parables of Jesus to the medieval mystery and passion plays, and from the rise of the modern novel to motion pictures and television, storytelling has transcended government, culture and philosophy.

Every great civilization has creation stories and tales of great exploits that define their moral universe. *The Odyssey, The Iliad, The Bible, Beowulf* and *The Mahabharata* are seminal stories that identify the personalities of various cultures and define their reason for being. The way stories are told has changed over the centuries, but the stories themselves have not lost their meaning or importance in people's lives.

There is no question that today the media has added an explosive element to the story. The statistics are unrelenting:

- 99 percent of households in America have at least one television.
- There are 2.24 television sets in the average American household.
- The average household watches television 5 hours and 11 minutes per day.
- By the time a young person is 18 years old, he or she will have watched 150,000 violent acts on television.
- 67 percent of Americans watch television while they eat dinner.

As a result, when asked, 54 percent of four- to six-year-olds prefer to watch television than spend time with their fathers.[3]

And that's just television.

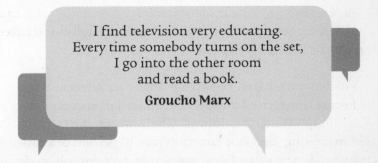

I find television very educating.
Every time somebody turns on the set,
I go into the other room
and read a book.
Groucho Marx

Today, more and more media platforms are competing with television for priority in our lives. Personal computers, social media, email, instant messaging, mobile devices and more are slicing up our lives into digital compartments, and their power has become frightening.

The *Los Angeles Times* reported on a study that indicated that one-third of Korean high school students make as many as 90 cell phone calls per day.[4] The study also linked high cell phone use to rates of depression.

I've stopped trying to keep up with the stats for the millions of eBay, Craigslist and other users. But I did notice that as of March 2012, Apple has now passed 25 *billion* downloads from the App Store. I spoke at a conference recently with Kevin Kelly, the cofounder of *Wired Magazine*. Kevin told me that researchers note that when toddlers are given a traditional photograph, they take their fingers and try to squeeze it to zoom in or out like a mobile screen. Today, even babies seem to be wired to understand the digital world!

An eight-year-old today sees the Internet with about as much fascination as you see the toilet.

Dean Kamen
Inventor of the Segway

According to James Twitchell, professor of English and advertising at the University of Florida:

> Much of our shared knowledge about ourselves and our culture comes to us through a commercial process of storytelling called "branding." The process starts early. A marketing professor estimates that 10 percent of a two-year-old's nouns are brand names. And an English study estimates that one out of every four babies speaks a brand name as a first word.[5]

This book isn't about the horrors of media, advertising or entertainment. There are plenty of books, scholarly journals and research out there that will make your hair stand on end when it comes to that subject. Does media violence beget real violence? Is the media responsible for the dumbing down of America? Has visual literacy displaced reading skills in schools? Are ebooks making us stupid? The questions go on and on, and by one count, more than 4,000 studies have been completed just on the effects of TV on children alone.

This book takes a different approach. The fact is that we're immersed in a media-driven culture. Our alarm goes off in the morning playing music from our favorite radio station or iPod; we get up and turn on the morning news to see what's happening in the world. We read the newspaper—most likely on a mobile device—over breakfast. We listen to the car broadcast or satelitte radio, music CD or a podcast on the way to work. We spend the day at our desk working by computer, periodically checking our email or stock prices on our mobile device or updating our social media pages. We listen to the radio on the way home. We watch the evening news over dinner. We catch our favorite TV programs in prime time or use the DVR to watch them when we choose, then take a last peek at our email, Facebook, Twitter or Pinterest, or check in online at eBay. Then we watch the "eyewitness news" right before we hit the sack, and maybe a few minutes of a popular late-night talk show.

And during that day, how many billboards, bus stop ads, Web banner ads, magazine layouts, and other media messages did you encounter? As I edit this page of the manuscript, I'm using a ballpoint pen with a hotel advertisement on its side.

Nearly every waking moment of our lives intersects with the media in some way. And although that much exposure can't be a good thing, the momentum is strong. So while we can't stop it, we at least need to understand it.

More than Just a Connection

We speak the language of Christianity, but we also speak the language of media. I don't believe there's simply a connection between branding and religion; I believe that religious experience is what the core of branding is all about.

As someone who has spent a lifetime sharing his faith with others, I have something to say about the influence that faith has on issues of personal identity, value and the search for meaning. Whether you're a nonbeliever investigating information on how to use branding to make your product connect more deeply with a customer, or a believer wondering how to expose your idea, project, church or ministry to a greater audience, this book will provide real answers.

The New Media World

Mass media has changed in a way that no one expected. In fact, I predict that our lifetime will be remembered as the era when "mass" media died. The truth is, it has been murdered. The suspects include digital music and video players, broadband Internet connections, social media, blogging and online entertainment.

Today, media is about *personalization*. The mass audience isn't interested in the same thing anymore. And they want their media customized. On my iPod and iPhone, I have classic rock and roll, bluegrass, praise and worship, Frank Sinatra, Southern gospel and even opera. I'm not interested in what radio stations *think* I need; now I can customize my own play list.

So what does this mean for those of us interested in sharing our faith or selling products through the media?

It means that it's time to wake up to the change.

In the church, pastors, Christian leaders and broadcasters always thought they had the answers to what their audience wanted and, more important, the audience would listen. Today the *audience* is in charge. In a virtually unlimited channel universe, with millions of online and mobile options, the audience has more choices than ever before; for us to justify their attention, we need to get on their wavelength.

The twenty-first century is changing everything about how to get your message to an audience. Yesterday it was about dumping the same message on the mass audience because they didn't have much choice. Today it's about making a connection—the kind of connection that not only makes them want to hear what you have to say, but also makes them respond.

> ## It doesn't matter if you have a great message if no one is listening.

Understanding that connection is a critical step in finding your audience.

Take Your **Thinking Deeper**

1. What are the things in your life for which you've felt intense loyalty? It could be people, organizations, causes or even products. Why did you have such intense feelings then (or still have such feelings now)?

2. How has technology personally impacted your life in the last decade? Has it changed the way you engage with real people?

3. Do you ever feel "addicted" to your mobile device, email or other technology?

4. Overall, do you think the power of major brands has grown in your lifetime? Do you feel this a good thing or bad thing?

5. Some say Christianity is about 10 to 15 years behind the technology curve. Why do you think that happens?

6. Do you think people of faith should do a better job using media and technology to share their story with the culture? Why does it matter?

7. How about you? Are you frustrated that your story isn't getting out there? What specifically is the greatest obstacle to you, your cause, or your product getting noticed?

The Influence of a Compelling Brand

> If the business were split up,
> I would take the brands, trademarks,
> and goodwill, and you could have
> all the bricks and mortar—and I would
> do better than you.
>
> **John Stuart**
> Former Chairman of Quaker Oats Corporation

Even today, "branding" could be the single most misunderstood term in all of American business. A visit to the business book section of a local bookstore will reveal an amazing number of titles: *Brand Leadership, Building Strong Brands, A Brand New World, Branded Nation, Brand Warfare, Strategic Brand Management, Be Your Own Brand, The 22 Immutable Laws of Branding, Brand Asset Management, Managing Brand Equity,* and many more. That tidal wave of branding titles causes many executives to look to branding as a magic bullet that will solve all their marketing headaches.

There's no question that branding has made a deep impact on the culture. In a world where Ronald McDonald is the most recognized man in America and the golden arches are more familiar than the Red Cross; where highway billboards display a Nike swoosh with no text or pictures; and one of the most popular mobile apps in Hollywood is the Starbucks locator, something is definitely up.

But what exactly is branding?

At its core, branding is simply the art of surrounding a product, organization or person with a powerful and compelling story. Just as you can brand a product like Nike or Starbucks, you can also brand organizations like churches, nonprofit groups and individuals. Even after the end of her daytime TV show, Oprah still has one of the most widely recognized personal brands in America, and she's very careful about controlling her look, style and the public's perception. I recently did a television commercial, and we wanted to use some still photographs of Oprah. I discovered just how difficult it was to get permission to use her image. She understands the power of a compelling brand and has become very astute at influencing every aspect of how she is perceived.

But how did this come about? How did the "story" about a product become more important than the product itself?

It's all about competition and the need to distinguish the product from the rest of the pack. At its most basic level, branding provides answers to the simple human need to differentiate one thing from another. Our present concept of branding came from cattle drives and the need to brand cows to maintain ownership. Things haven't changed that much from the time of pressing red-hot iron into the flesh of herds of cattle to monogramming a little horse and rider on a Ralph Lauren dress shirt (worn by herds of businessmen).

Before the industrial revolution in this country, there was pretty much one brand of soap, one type of sugar, one kind of bread. It was a simple world back then, but it was also a world without variety. In those days, most products were handmade, and the first to the market usually won the day.

As a result, life was defined by social class, nationality, race, politics, religion or the essential needs of life, such as food, clothing, shelter and sex.

But the industrial revolution gave inventors and business leaders the ability to create a massive surplus. It also paved the way for more competition, as more and more companies were able to create their own versions of products.

As a result, our lives burst out of the classifications and identities we had held for centuries and changed our focus to the wide variety of products hitting the shelves. Thus, for the first time, you could be known for the car you drove, the brand of suit you wore, the perfume you used or the games you played. As the consumer culture caught hold, we could identify ourselves with a virtually unlimited range of goods and services to the point that today we proudly wear Armani suits, carry a Prada handbag, wear a Rolex watch, drive an Audi or drink Starbucks coffee.

My wife, Kathleen, and I recently attended a wedding in Palm Springs, California. What we didn't realize was that the wedding was scheduled for the same weekend as a motorcycle rally that brought 30,000 bikers to the streets of that desert city.

Watching the thousands of bikers that weekend, I was reminded of the tremendous power of the Harley-Davidson brand. "Harleys" were easily the overwhelming choice among the bikers, but loyalty to their beloved brand didn't stop with the motorcycles. They also sported Harley-Davidson leather jackets, helmets, hats, headscarves, gloves, saddlebags, T-shirts, chaps, and more. Stores featured Harley-Davidson children's clothing and women's lingerie.

As I talked to a few of the bikers, I realized that the ultimate conceit is how they consider themselves "outsiders," "rebels" and "independents." Some told me they felt they were the last real outlaws and freethinkers left on the planet. They weren't loyal to anything but themselves, and they relished the kind of freedom they felt people like me couldn't possibly enjoy.

As they enthusiastically shared with me about how independent they felt, they were sitting on a Harley-Davidson motorcycle and wearing all the branded clothes that came with it. With one biker, I couldn't find a single item of clothing he wore that didn't have the company logo on it somewhere.

In truth, while they imagined themselves as rebels, they were actually committed worshipers at the altar of the Harley-Davidson brand.

In a nonprofit or religious environment, the process isn't much different. You may be a pastor wanting to make a more significant impression in your community, a media ministry reaching out to a larger support base, a missions organization attempting to raise funding, or a museum trying to raise your profile in a geographic region.

> Simply because in a world that is bewildering in terms of competitive clamor, in which rational choice has become almost impossible, brands represent clarity, reassurance, consistency, status, membership–everything that enables human beings to help define themselves. Brands represent identity.
>
> **Wally Olins**
> Chairman of Saffron Brand Consultants

You may be writing a book, producing a film, pitching a Web company or launching a new business. Whatever the purpose, the goal is to win the hearts and minds of the largest audience possible and imprint an indelible story around your vision.

The power of these stories and the hold they exert over our lives is remarkable, and many would say the power of story is embedded in our genetic makeup. From the ancient days of the Israelite storytellers who recited the epic chronicles of Abraham, Isaac and Jacob, to the writers, preachers and filmmakers of today, we are a story-driven people, and we use stories to make sense of life.

It's no surprise that the most watched television programs, year after year, are situation comedies, episodic dramas and movies—all story-driven formats. Even reality programming needs a story to drive the momentum forward. Whether it's danger, conflict, family tension or competition, the stories captured in reality television simply continue an ancient tradition (perhaps with a little weirdness tossed in as well).

Stories work because we want to experience the emotions, feelings and passions of others who have encountered the challenges we face each day. We love to see a hero prevail and a bad guy get his due; and we love to weep with a tragic loss.

> In 1954, the year of my birth,
> TV dinners, I love Lucy and the H-bomb
> were invented; and to this day, I'm not sure
> if there was a connection.

The year I was born, Decca Records recorded rock 'n' roll's first real smash hit, "Shake, Rattle and Roll"; Elvis Presley made his first record; and Walt Disney went on television. TV was exploding, and Walt Disney was one of the first to realize the magnetic power of a compelling brand.

When the *Davy Crockett* program debuted on national television, I had to have a coonskin cap, a pioneer rifle and the leather outfit that completed the look. I had a Davy Crockett lunchbox, T-shirt, pencil and belt, and I was ready for attacks from Indians, raging bears or my little sister. If my mother had not forced me to take off my coonskin cap at bedtime, I would have worn it 24/7.

I wanted to be Davy Crockett; and even though I was a young child, I adopted his story as my own.

Eventually, I did the same with Superman, Batman, the Green Hornet, James Bond, and others—all because I loved the stories.

I saw my two daughters do the same thing with all the Disney princesses. Both of my daughters had Snow White dresses, and they literally wore them until they disintegrated. Long after they had become virtual rags, those dresses were still our daughters' favorites. My girls were hypnotized by the story of the princess who was cast out, who never gave up and eventually found her prince.

During Jesus' short time of ministry on earth, He had to teach a message that wouldn't simply change people during His lifetime, but transform the world for ages to come. If you had faced that challenge, what would you have done?

Stories have remarkable power, which is exactly the reason Jesus used them.

Most pastors I know would start with a mission statement. Then they would outline their doctrinal principles and statement of faith. Then they would find a building, preferably one with good parking and the ability to expand. Then, realizing the need to leave a legacy in the faith, they would start working on their theology and perhaps throw in a handful of leadership principles and church-growth tips. Then they'd be ready.

It's worth asking the question on the famous bracelets: WWJD? (What would Jesus do?)

Jesus did what many pastors in that position would probably consider a real career killer: He started telling stories. And He told stories that He didn't even explain. Sometimes He would enlighten the disciples in private, but rarely did He say the words in public, "Now let me tell you what that story means."

Plus, the stories weren't that profound. They didn't involve kings or princes, wars or major conflict, and they certainly weren't particularly deep. All the wonderful elements that make great legends were left out. There weren't even any epic tales of heroes and damsels in distress.

Most of Jesus' stories were just everyday people doing everyday things. They weren't particularly exciting, romantic or even thrilling.

Why was Jesus ready to risk only three years of ministry by telling simple stories?

Stories drill deeply into your brain and explode later with meaning. Sometimes the meaning comes when you least expect it. Stories impact audiences because each person interprets the story in light of his or her own personal situation and experience. As a result, the impact is far greater than a simple object lesson or teaching session.

> Morpheus said it best in the blockbuster
> movie *The Matrix.* He described it as a
> "splinter in your mind."

I'm reminded of the power of the *Andy Griffith Show*, possibly the greatest comedy series ever filmed. Andy could disarm any situation by simply telling a story.

In many cases, you can interchangeably use the words "brand," "story," "identity" and, sometimes, "reputation." Branding is about building trust and loyalty and extending your customer relationships far beyond a single transaction.

My father was a pastor who owned a 7,000-volume library. He was also an amateur historian. So, in addition to a vast number of books on theology and Christian studies, many of those volumes were about the Civil War and World War II. My father hit the beach with the First Marine Division in the Pacific at Guadalcanal, and his unit slugged their way through heavy enemy fire and tremendous losses to take the island for the Allies. It was a key wartime position for an airfield, and although it was a bloody campaign, it was to become a critical staging point against the Japanese.

Like most men who fought in World War II, the memory has remained remarkably vivid throughout his life. As a result, he built a massive collection of books on the Pacific campaign. He was born into a mill family that for generations had labored folding sheets and towels, or worked their fingers to the bone at looms in colossal North Carolina cotton mills. But the war broke that cycle and gave my father a way out. As quickly as he could, he grabbed the opportunity and enlisted, and he never looked back. After the war, he attended college and, eventually, graduate school. As a pastor, he had four master's degrees and two doctorates. Education was my father's way out of poverty. He taught me that learning was incredibly valuable.

But among those 7,000 books in his library collection, I don't think my father ever owned a single novel.

He believed that if it wasn't "true," it was a waste of time. As a result, I never understood the power of fiction until I attended college myself. That was when I discovered that some stories might not be *true,* but they expressed *Truth* with a capital T. Stories help us define who we are, where we came from and where we are going. Stories are like a compass to help us find our bearings, and they provide a place of belonging.

That's why stories have become the central focus of the art of branding; and that's how branding has become such a powerful force.

Take Your **Thinking Deeper**

1. What are the top three brands you are most loyal to today? Why?

2. Why do you think stories and storytellers are such an important part of our culture?

3. What was the most powerful brand or advertising image you remember from childhood?

4. When it comes to movies, do you view more dramas, or documentaries? How about TV? Do you watch reality programming more than movies or dramas? What about books—do you read more fiction or more nonfiction?

5. Reflecting back in time, how have stories impacted your life?

> Science is nothing but perception.
> **Plato**

> It is the function of art to renew our perception. What we are familiar with we cease to see. The writer shakes up the familiar scene, and, as if by magic, we see a new meaning in it.
> **Anaïs Nin**
> Avant-garde Novelist

The Power of Perception

(Why Perception Is Just as Important as Reality)

The key to effective branding is that a successful brand isn't what *you* say it is; it's what *they* say it is. For instance, it doesn't matter if the local food bank is the best in the nation if a rumor starts that states it's giving away tainted produce. It won't matter that you're a brilliant pastor if your congregation thinks you're a hack. And it certainly won't matter that a humanitarian organization is global if nobody's ever heard of it.

In other words, it's about *perception*.

Telling an effective story about your church, ministry, project, idea or yourself begins with understanding the power of perception. In a media-driven culture, perception can be even more important than reality because, in an instant-message, texting and email culture, word travels fast. Whether it's a simple email message that is continually forwarded exponentially to everyone in your address book, a viral video that's distributed though the Web, or the convenience of mobile phones, in the digital age, it's tough to keep a lid on bad news, as various American presidents have discovered with White House leaks.

I often tell about my first real experience of understanding the power of perception. I was in my early twenties and had the opportunity to lead a film crew to the headwaters of the Amazon River in Brazil to film the work of a medical relief team. It was an exciting opportunity, but I had no idea of the challenge I would face trying to get our film equipment through customs in the Brazilian city of Manaus. The city is located about 1,000 miles upriver from the Atlantic and today is a beautiful city of nearly 2 million people. When we arrived at the airport, which in those days had been literally carved out of the jungle, I had a three-man crew and a number of large cases of film equipment that had to be cleared through customs.

I've filmed in nearly 50 countries around the world. I've survived military coups in Africa, been chased by Communist sympathizers in the Caribbean, lived with Nomads in the deserts of the Middle East, bribed corrupt customs officials to release equipment (and sometimes my people), and a host of other strange and sometimes dangerous situations; but I was not ready for the unusual response I received from one particular customs official as we were trying to get into Brazil.

"Can you prove you're a filmmaker from the United States?" he asked.

I had my passport, customs documentation and equipment lists, but I've never actually been asked to prove what I do for a living. After all, it's not like we carry a membership card or diploma around to prove we're in some type of "filmmaker's club."

"Well, I'm sorry, Mr. Cooke. Until you can prove to me you're actually an official filmmaker from the United States, I can't allow your equipment into the country. You're welcome to come in, but I'll have to keep your equipment locked here in customs until you can provide adequate documentation."

Official filmmaker?! It was insane. It's not as if tourists carry hundreds of thousands of dollars of film and video equipment on vacation. We argued and argued, but nothing worked. I took the crew to the hotel, frustrated and upset, because we still had airplane flights, boat charters and numerous other connections to meet; and now everything was being thrown into chaos. We paced the hotel room, tried to make phone calls and discussed every possible solution, but we came up empty.

The jungle heat and humidity didn't help. Every day we would travel back to the customs official and request the equipment, and every day he would turn us down. Quietly, we even offered him a bribe, since that technique had worked in plenty of other places; but no dice, he was an honest guy and he just wouldn't budge.

After a few days, we considered returning to the United States in failure, knowing that we had wasted thousands of dollars to get this far, with nothing to show for it.

The problem was **perception**.

It might have been because we were so young to be in possession of that kind of gear, but no matter how many passports, equipment lists and travel arrangements we showed the customs official, for some reason he was convinced that we weren't actual filmmakers. We argued until we were exhausted, but his *perception* just wouldn't change.

Finally, after four days of haggling and arguing, I walked angrily back to my room, knowing that we had tried everything and still failed. When I started to undress for the night, I pulled my wallet out of my jeans pocket and for some reason decided to flip through the back section where I kept my insurance cards and driver's license; that's when the card that would change everything fell out.

Years before, a nonprofit organization in Hollywood began publishing a magazine devoted to filmmaking called *American Film*. It was a wonderful magazine for anyone who truly loved movies, because it wasn't a trendy publication about movie stars. It featured real articles about the behind-the-scenes process of making films and included intimate interviews, interesting stories and other information about the industry. The magazine was a highly respected division of an organization still in existence today called the American Film Institute, which conducts classes and workshops for serious filmmakers and sponsors major industry events.

At that time, when you signed up for a subscription to the magazine, you received a membership card into the American Film Institute. It didn't really mean anything more than the magazine subscription, except that it might get you into an occasional film screening or movie premiere.

When the American Film Institute magazine subscription card fell out of my wallet, it gave me a brilliant idea. The next morning, we were back in the customs official's office.

"You want proof that we are filmmakers from the United States, right?"

"That's correct," he replied, "and so far, I've seen nothing."

I whipped out my AFI card. Fortunately, the information on the card about the magazine subscription was printed on the back in very small letters, and I hoped he wouldn't notice.

"I'm a member of the American Film Institute." I pointed at the front. "There, you can see my name printed on my membership card."

The customs official looked at the card carefully, compared the signature with my passport, and then a light switched on in his head. His demeanor changed, and suddenly he jumped to his feet grinning like a car salesman who has just made a deal.

"Why didn't you tell me you were a member of the American Film Institute?" He beamed with excitement, as if he'd stumbled on a real celebrity. He had no idea what the AFI was, but it sure sounded impressive.

"Welcome to our country! Please enjoy your filming!"

He walked around the desk, embraced everyone on my crew and then led us into the warehouse where customs was holding our equipment. He couldn't have been nicer. The next thing we knew we were given a police escort with full sirens and lights back to the hotel, with government employees personally carrying our equipment and unloading it for us.

I kissed my AFI membership card, carefully tucked it away in my wallet and carried it faithfully for years, even after the actual magazine ceased publication. The simple magazine subscription card meant nothing in itself, but it completely changed the perception of that customs official. When his perception changed, we went from being tourists at best (con artists at worst) to being celebrated filmmakers from the United States, deserving official government approval and support.

In more than 35 years of active work in the entertainment and media industries, I've seen few situations where perception played such an important role. The influence of the mass media in our culture is changing everything, and "perception" is the language spoken by modern media. In a world where sound bites heavily influence the political process, the unique characteristics of mass media now affect every aspect of our lives. Public relations has become an art form as companies and organizations (and even celebrities) confront the need to impact and hopefully control public opinion. Perception has become a critical part of advertising campaigns, press releases and public statements.

As a producer, director and media consultant in Hollywood, perception is my business. I deal in the visual world of products and people and how they are perceived by the viewing audience. Today, in a media-saturated culture, perception is the currency of commerce.

As a person of faith in the industry, I've spent years wrestling with the moral implications of perception. In watching tobacco companies position cigarettes as non-addictive, casino owners position themselves as family entertainment, and pornographers position themselves as champions of free speech, I looked at the art of perception as a negative, deceitful proposition.

Indeed it can be; but like many things, I learned that it also has a flip side as I began to study how Jesus went to great lengths to impact the public perception of His ministry and His purpose on the earth.

Was Jesus a Brand Manager?

Jesus came to earth in a different way than people expected. They wanted a king; He was born into poverty.

He preached a different message than people expected. They wanted a revolution; He preached a message of love.

When one of His best friends was dying, Jesus—against the wishes of His friends—took His time getting to Lazarus.

He healed a man and then told him not to tell anyone.

He carefully chose the men who would be His closest associates.

During the height of His popularity, He withdrew to remote places to be alone.

He chose the method of His triumphal entry into Jerusalem.

When He could have escaped in the garden of Gethsemane, He told Peter to stop fighting and quietly allowed Himself to be arrested.

During the events that led to His execution, He even controlled Pilate's interrogation of Him by only responding to certain questions.

Jesus had a purpose and plan for His life, and He refused to let others determine His destiny or how He would be perceived.

Someone once said that if you don't control your perception, you'll live the rest of your life at the mercy of others who will.

Who will write the story of your life? Will you leave your own legacy or wait for others to create it for you?

Celebrity Culture

The global fascination with celebrities has been an important element in the realization of how important perception is today. For instance, with the advent of the relatively recent concept of "celebrity," the basis of fame has undergone a striking change. In the past, a person became famous for accomplishing a significant task, such as making a great discovery, winning the championship football game or finding the cure for a deadly disease. Today, just being in the news makes someone famous; actual accomplishment really isn't necessary anymore. A movie star shows up at a party and makes front-page news; high-profile sexual affairs propel some to national TV interviews and book deals; and paparazzi photographers have made celebrity "journalism" the foundation of entire magazines.

How many celebrities today have no talent, job skills or abilities? Many have never had a real job and have never accomplished anything of significance, and yet they're the focus of celebrity journalism night after night in Hollywood. Featured at major industry parties, some are sought-after guests (and are actually paid just to show up) because of their ability to attract attention.

Advertising Has Changed

That's also an interesting aspect of why the advertising industry has moved from "informational" advertising to "emotional" advertising. In the beginning of modern media, the primary goal of marketers was to tell the public about the wonderful features of a product—how it works, the quality of the construction or the helpful features. Today, advertisers don't tell us *about* the product; they tell us *how we're going to feel* when we use the product. When was the last time you saw an athletic shoe commercial that described the high-quality materials that went into the shoes, the excellent construction or its useful features? Today, the focus is on convincing you that when you strap on those shoes, you'll suddenly leap like an all-star, win championship sports events or fit in with a cooler crowd.

In the same way, beer advertising tells you very little about the distinguishing qualities of a particular brand or the high-level ingredients that went into the process. Instead they show you how that brand of beer will make you look and feel cool. You'll meet beautiful women at great parties and suddenly become more desirable and attractive to the opposite sex. It happens in nearly any product area you care to choose.

It's not about facts anymore; it's about **perception**.

Who You Are Is Important, but How You're Perceived Is Critical

In today's media-saturated culture, who you are becomes less important than how you're perceived. When researchers study the process of communication, they realize that the message being sent is not always the message being received. For a variety of reasons, few communicated messages actually arrive with the same intentions, information and impact.

"Perception" is a powerful word and has enormous consequences.

How can we use perception in our church, ministry or nonprofit organization? How can we use it to increase our influence? To what extent can we control the way the culture perceives us, and how can we use those techniques to make change happen and accomplish our goals? First, we need to understand that perception can be a positive tool.

The Positive Side of Perception

Too many religious believers view the perception issue as a negative tool of manipulation and refuse to consider its positive potential. I've had the opportunity to teach these principles around the world, and one of my favorite places to lecture is Russia, where I've taught media and broadcasting techniques in Moscow and St. Petersburg. When you study the history of Communism in the former Soviet Union, you'll find that Lenin was a master of perception, and he used these techniques in a negative way to keep millions of people under the brutal hand of the Soviet state. Lenin always felt that cinema was the greatest art form, because he understood the power of movies to inspire, motivate and educate. Under his control, the Russian film industry grew at an enormous rate but was used as a terrible tool to help subjugate the Russian people for decades.

In our home, we've mounted a large Soviet-era political poster promoting the use of cinema, which I found in a Moscow antiques market. The poster features an actress in a highly dramatic pose. The quote in the Russian language is from Lenin himself: "Of all the arts, cinema is the greatest."

In spite of its abuse, the power of perception can be utilized for good if we know how to activate it in our lives. The way to do that is to consider your audience before crafting your message.

Start Thinking in Reverse

It's not the message you send but the message that's received that counts. It doesn't matter how brilliant your sermons are; if your intention is misunderstood by the listener, then you've failed to communicate. That's why I always prefer to start at the receiving end first to make sure my message has the best chance of being received properly. How do I do it? I first consider my audience. I know that every listener is evaluating my message through his or her own framework of life experiences and cultural background, which dictate to a great extent the impact the message will have on him or her.

When it comes to delivering your message—even jokes—know who you're dealing with, and know them as intimately as possible. Whatever your business, make sure you tailor your product, presentation or message to your particular audience. Your approach for selling ice should be dramatically different depending on whether you're selling to nomads in the desert or Inuits at the North Pole.

Don't begin with your message; begin with your audience. Think how they could perceive your comments and all the myriad ways they might relate to its content. Then start preparing your message.

The Importance of Packaging

When I was a kid, television meant choosing between three channels. Whoopee. Today, our children have virtually an unlimited number of channels. The difference between yesterday and today is extraordinary and very important to the way you present your message.

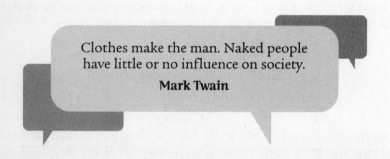

Clothes make the man. Naked people have little or no influence on society.
Mark Twain

My producing experience in an unlimited-channel universe indicates that people take less than five seconds to decide to watch your TV program. That's it. Think about how quickly you handle a TV remote and how little chance you give each program to grab your attention. Audiences today are sophisticated and aren't willing to put up with boring production or low-quality pictures. Therefore, I always advise my media clients that how a program is packaged is just as important as its content. For instance, no matter how brilliant the program content might be, it has to be packaged in a high-quality, contemporary and compelling way. Otherwise, the viewer won't watch long enough to hear the content, and that means you've lost your audience.

Packaging simply means the "package" (or presentation) that a program is wrapped around. For example, is the lighting interesting? How about the music? Are the graphics contemporary? What about the editing style? Is it well directed and acted? All of these elements, and more, combined create a powerful package.

In the same way, you, your church or ministry, your media outreach, your business or your idea needs an exciting package in order to be perceived as powerfully as possible. For instance, I've always been fascinated with how quickly store clerks jump to my attention when I'm wearing a suit, and how slowly they react when I'm in jeans or casual clothes. Don't become a clothing snob and use clothes to elevate yourself above others; no one respects a peson in the office who uses clothes as a label to separate himself or herself from everyone else. But do know and learn the power of how to dress appropriately and how clothes can be used to give you access to people, places and events.

Make sure you have finished speaking before your audience has finished listening.

Dorothy Sarnoff

Opera Singer

Well-dressed British dandy Beau Brummell said, "If people turn to look at you on the street, you are not well dressed." He believed in the power of subtlety, and I wish more pastors and hosts of faith-based television programs today listened to his advice.

Many people would say that the ability to speak publicly is a critical skill. In the pulpit, managing a board meeting, leading a team, addressing the employees or speaking to the public are all important leadership skills focused on the ability to communicate effectively.

The bottom line? Who you are is important, but you can never underestimate the value of how you are perceived.

Take Your **Thinking Deeper**

1. Think about a situation in your experience where perception was reality for you.

2. When meeting someone for the first time, have you ever jumped to a wrong conclusion about that person based on your initial perception?

3. Do you agree that Jesus cared about His perception? Either way, explain why.

4. How do you think celebrities have impacted today's culture? Where do you see celebrity influence in politics and other places where it didn't exist before? Is this a good thing? Explain.

5. How should you consider perception, and how can it positively influence your own career, church or a cause you care about?

6. How is your own organization "packaged"? How effective are your website, print materials and other expressions of your message?

> Brands are belief systems.
> **Patrick Hanlon**

> In some cases this is so powerful that the brand becomes more than a brand, and it becomes a way of life.
> **Martin Lindstrom**

A New Religion?

There's a new school of thought within the branding and marketing community that has connected successful branding with the features of religious belief; that is, traits that are intrinsic to religious belief—a sense of belonging, the feeling of community, the collective rituals, the shared belief system now point to branding becoming a type of religious experience in America. While that concept might be difficult to swallow for a person of serious religious faith, it does present some intriguing parallels that are difficult to ignore. In many ways, corporate America is subtly attempting to replace religion with branding, at least in the West. In past eras, we might have thought of ourselves in terms of our religious community; but today, Methodist, Baptist, Assembly of God or Lutheran affiliations have given way to Ralph Lauren, Diesel or Lexus.

Just yesterday, I overheard a conversation between two businessmen about watches. After comparing their very expensive timepieces, one of the men said, "Well, I've just always thought of myself as a Rolex man." To which the other replied, "I think I'm more of a Breitling man myself." Whatever criteria they used to define a "Rolex man" or a "Breitling man," you can be sure it was based on a very strategic advertising strategy by two companies that understand the power of branding.

Today, brands are the tool for defining our place in the culture, and they have given our capitalist society markers for determining who we are, where we belong and our status in relation to others.

Branding helps us express ourselves to the greater community of believers. Knowing that a friend is a Levi's person or a Nike person helps us understand who they are and what values they represent. Target is the store that sells "mass with class" because it represents high fashion on a limited budget. In a similar way, IKEA has touched a nerve with young couples looking for hip, contemporary furniture without the hefty price tag. Walk into a J. Crew store and you'll see a very defined idea of what that customer is like.

In fact, truly successful brands give the impression that there is simply no substitute for what they offer, whether it's a service, product or company. A particular brand becomes a must-have in the minds of the public.

Brand communicates ideas, values and standards. What was expressed a generation ago through religious affiliation is now communicated through what we wear, the car we drive and the pen that sits in our pocket.

To a secular culture, brands and religion have merged.

The truth is, savvy marketers and advertisers have tapped into our global human aspirations for a sense of belonging, value, meaning and worship, and have turned ordinary, everyday products into brands—and eventually, brands into religions.

In a secular society, brands are worshiped as gods. We value them, express loyalty to them and associate with others of like-minded belief. In major American cities, people have been killed for designer handbags, athletic shoes or jeans. The right brands are sometimes coveted more than human life; and at the altar of validation, blood can be spilled as a sacrifice to the trendy.

The Age of the Brandasaurus

By now, you might be getting slightly uncomfortable with the idea of branding. There's no question there is a dark side to the world of the brand, and critics of branding are legion. Brands have distorted the buying and selling of goods and services, hyping products based not on intrinsic usefulness or value, but on desire alone. Branding has perpetuated the buying and selling of our young people through commercial manipulation and distortion. It has created global corporations whose products are manufactured in Asian sweatshops by underage children making pennies a day. And it has distorted our priorities, making us believe that without this or that product, our lives will be meaningless and empty.

Sometimes it's hard to argue with critics like Naomi Klein, author of *No Logo*, who calls our culture "The Age of the Brandasaurus."

But there are two different things working here: (1) the power of creating a compelling story around a product, organization or person, and (2) the unethical business practices of corporations around the world. As companies build their organizations into global behemoths, they often trade their integrity for the ability to mass market products. As a person of faith, there is no middle ground in our battle to help everyone reach a standard of living that allows him or her to move out of poverty. Any breach of that standard—whether it be exploiting workers, taking advantage of employees or breaking the law—is out of the question. Without sounding too spiritual, the more we help create decent working and living environments for people, the more we become the people God intends us to be.

I believe that we can understand and use the principles of branding without resorting to corporate dishonesty. As branding expert Wally Olins suggests:

> The weakness of the Naomi Klein school of anti-capitalists is to treat brands as though their only manifestation is corporate and commercial. The influence, strategies and tactics of branding now go way beyond this. Branding is playing a large and increasing part in politics, the nation, sports, culture, and the volunteer sector.[1]

And I would add the "religious" world as well. Telling the story about a product and how it interacts and connects with a consumer doesn't have to be a debasing or dehumanizing experience. The key is in understanding how the media works and using it with integrity and authenticity.

Branding as Meaning

In *Consuming Faith: Integrating Who We Are with What We Buy,* Tom Beaudoin wrote:

> I try to show that one reason the brand economy "works" is that it brings a similar sort of meaningful order and coherence to people's lives that classic spiritual disciplines did in the past (and still do for some today). This is not to make apologies for the brand economy, but to show that it is a spiritual force to be reckoned with, and that people are not idiotic dupes of advertisers but soulfully hungry persons looking for a way to bring a sense of meaningful discipline to their lives. Maybe the brand economy and traditional spiritual disciplines have some things to learn from each other.[2]

Bringing meaning to life is one of the reasons I'm so passionate about branding and helping others understand how they can use these principles to reach today's culture. Frankly, the Church has often done a poor job of communicating with the culture, and it often comes from not understanding what questions fill the public's mind.

> ## Too many religious leaders are answering questions the culture isn't asking.

Most people today don't understand our evangelical language (what does "born again" mean?), don't care about our priorities (the Ten Commandments in schools?), and certainly don't follow our rules (the Bible). As a result, I see pastors engage the culture using Scripture to support their arguments even though their opponents don't recognize the Bible as authoritative. They use religious language even though the audience has no clue what the words mean. And we've lost touch with how we're perceived by the culture—all of which cause the culture to simply dismiss us as out of touch or, worse, consider us nuts.

When I was growing up, the vast majority of people in our community respected the church; even if they didn't attend, they honored Christian values and generally had a biblical worldview.

That's not the case anymore. While we're busy having in-house theological arguments, the culture has already passed us by. As Paul did in Acts 17, to engage a post-Christian culture, we need to speak in a language they understand, respect their values (even if we don't agree with them) and be compelling enough to justify their attention.

Just as important, no one in my experience was ever won to Christ through humiliation or embarrassment. So the next time you have a chance to ridicule a nonbeliever, think twice about its effectiveness.

As much as I'd love to go back to a world that respects and values Christian principles, the truth is, we live in occupied territory. If we're going to be successful in communicating a message of hope, we need to realize that the culture doesn't think the way we do. To make an impact, we must take the time and effort to understand, relate to and love the very people who may think we're crazy.

Telling that story effectively is the heart of branding.

The Tenets of "Brand Faith"

The more I study branding as it relates to nonprofits, churches and ministries, the more I'm drawn back to religion itself. Over and over, secular branding experts point to religious faith as the template for real branding. In his book *Primal Branding*, Patrick Hanlon, founder and CEO of Thinktopia, Inc., has discovered a remarkable parallel between branding and religious faith. In what Hanlon calls "The Primal Code," he finds seven points where successful branding and religion intersect.[3]

1. The Creation Story

Just like the great faiths of the world, every successful product needs a creation story. Whether it's the legendary story of Ray Kroc walking into a McDonald's Brothers restaurant and marveling at the food delivery system they created; a track coach using a waffle iron to create a revolutionary rubber sole for track shoes; or the secret recipe for Coke, a product's "creation story" holds a great mystery, fascination and attraction for most people.

It happens all the time in the Christian ministry world: Joyce Meyer starting out by conducting small meetings in motel banquet rooms with a beat-up rental trailer of books and teaching tapes; newspaper magnate William Randolph Hearst's command to "puff Graham" at the beginning of Billy Graham's ministry; Oral Roberts's healing from childhood tuberculosis; Joel Osteen's father, John, starting what would become the largest church in America in an abandoned feed store on Mother's Day 1959. These are all stories that capture the hearts and imagination of church members, ministry supporters and the public at large.

The creation story can be renewed as well from generation to generation. When Texas pastor John Osteen was nearing the end of his life, he begged his youngest son, Joel, to preach for him. Joel, having spent most of his life as his father's television producer, had no desire to preach, and he gently rebuffed his father time after time. Finally, as his dad was nearing death, Joel relented and agreed to preach one Sunday morning. After setting up a phone line so that his father could listen to the service live from the hospital, Joel preached his first sermon. What he didn't realize at the time was that it would also be the last sermon his father ever heard.

Joel went on to build Lakewood Church into the largest place of worship in the United States, and the story of his first sermon has become one of the fascinating anecdotes that surround the ministry.

What's your creation story? Have you kept it alive and in front of people?

Early in my career, I worked with evangelist Oral Roberts at the peak of his ministry when he was producing prime-time TV specials on national television. At the time, I grew weary of his constantly retelling the story of his healing from childhood tuberculosis and his calling into ministry. In the studio, I would tell him over and over, "Oral, give it a rest." But now, looking back, I understand his desire to keep the story in the forefront of his supporters' minds to let them know they were a part of a great ministry that was birthed inside a miracle.

As Patrick Hanlon teaches, creation stories tell the "who" and the "why" and give the consumer a basis for trust in the product. In your ministry, your creation story tells about God's calling, the foundation of your church or ministry, and the platform for your convictions.

2. The Creed

Just as the great religions have statements of faith, or sets of doctrinal beliefs, so too do great brands. "It's the real thing." "Save the Whales." "Just Do It." "Think Different." In each case, the words are more than a tagline; they become the rallying cry of the brand. A great tagline calls people to action, gives them a purpose and defines who they are. In the world of secular products, it might be a tagline that's used with advertising, or a private creed that motivates employees. Sometimes it is both.

Take the line for Absolut Vodka: "How big can we get before we get bad?" This question is not something you necessarily want the public to know, but it's a great motivating creed inside the company. Creeds call people to action, motivate employees and customers, and define who you are and why you exist.

3. The Icons

In Hanlon's world, icons are most often the logos of an organization or product. I'll talk about logos in detail later, but for now, a mark or logo is a simple visual expression of your brand. It's easy to recognize (think about the Nike swoosh) and it's simple to understand. Sometimes icons evolve from print and become larger, like the start-up "bong" on an Apple computer, or the Budweiser Clydesdale horses. Essentially, an icon is the simplest and most visual way to express your brand, your values and your essence to the customer.

Logos are highly misunderstood in the church and ministry world. To use a logo effectively, it has to be greater than a cute symbol. It must express in that simple package the essence of who you are and how you can change someone's life—a big challenge to be sure, but that's the goal.

What's the point? After a month of filming in Nigeria during a military coup; and after having a cameraman arrested and spending thousands in bribes to get him out; and after being hungry, dirty and exhausted, I can't adequately express the emotions I felt when I walked out on the airport concourse in Lagos and saw the AA logo on the tail of the American Airlines jet that was going to take me home.

How desperately have you looked for a Starbucks logo when traveling? The key to a logo is immediate recognition. If your logo is so cool and hip that no one knows what it is, you've failed. And if people love the design but don't understand the meaning of the logo, you've failed again.

4. The Rituals

Life is full of rituals—weddings, graduations, religious services, and more. But when it comes to consumer products, Hanlon believes that repeated interaction with a product or company creates an important ritual as well. In *Primal Branding*, Hanlon describes how companies like Unilever and General Motors have actually hired anthropologists to study the rituals involved with their products, whether it's the laundry process or driving a Chevy.

After the terrorist attacks of 9/11, the process of airline travel has become a massive ritual involving showing your ID, learning what we can and can't take on the plane, what to check as baggage, dealing with security screenings, waiting for the departure. Today airlines spend enormous amounts of time understanding the ritual and trying to make it as pleasant and quick as possible under the circumstances.

Rituals have been part of the fabric of religious experience since God told Adam and Eve how to live in the Garden. Since that time, the Church has developed elaborate rituals regarding worship, music and various forms of liturgy that have helped believers navigate the faith. Rituals give form to ideals and allow physical actions to convey meaning.

Although "high church" rituals are what most people think of when it comes to Christianity, the truth is, even the most contemporary service has repeated routines that help the congregation—from greeting the visitors, finding nursery facilities and joining the choir; to the educational programs of the church, small groups and helping your members understand and grow comfortable with these actions. All are a critical key to their involvement. It's not a matter of hiring an "efficiency expert" to make confusing routines simple and easy. The challenge is how to inject meaning into the rituals, making them part of the overall worship experience.

From a media ministry perspective, it's no different. How consumers contact your ministry, the way they navigate your website, order books and materials, attend conferences, or the many other encounters they may have with the organization, are all things to consider. It's not a matter of being slick; it's a matter of making it worth the trouble. Giving meaning to routine actions is what makes the difference.

5. The Pagans, or Nonbelievers
Hanlon's branding ideas also intersect with religious faith when it comes to nonbelievers. In the marketing world, he's talking about people who don't use the product: the "heathens" and "idolaters," as he calls them. (Heard those terms before?)

In the marketplace it's about Republicans and Democrats, pro-life and pro-choice, hawks and doves, health-food nuts and fast-food lovers, digital marketing and traditional retailing, New York and Los Angeles, drinkers and nondrinkers, smokers and nonsmokers, and on and on.

To define who you are, you must define who you aren't.

As Hanlon says, "We live in a world that has defined itself by contrast and paradox for thousands of years."[4] Traditionally, Christians have not been hesitant to point out sin in the culture, but lately, we see that happening less and less. To a great extent, that happened because society has turned away from preachers who hammer on them with messages about hell and damnation. As the culture locks itself into a "What's in it for me?" mentality, they obviously want to hear less and less about what they're doing wrong or what judgment might be waiting for them after this life.

I've traditionally been one to focus on the positive. I worry that if Christians continue to focus on the negative, we will become known as "the people who are against everything." When that happens, it becomes easier and easier for the culture to turn us off. But if Hanlon is correct, being clear about what we're against isn't always a bad thing.

As Sonny Arguinzoni, Jr., pastor of Victory Outreach, a ministry with a powerful reputation for reaching inner-city gang members, stated recently in *Christianity Today*: "You can't make the gospel look gray or shady when Jesus says: 'You have to leave this and follow me.'"[5]

I think the lesson here is that defining the nonbelievers isn't really about condemning them; it's about identifying them. Once we can define who the nonbelievers are, we can better focus on the options for reaching that particular audience. That's why doctrinal ignorance can be so damaging. In order to express our message properly, we need to believe the right things. In a world where far too many pastors discount a strong theological education, we're developing a generation of pastors who are ignorant of the basic principles of the faith. As a result, we don't know who we are, and we certainly can't identify who we aren't.

One of the big alarms that Philip Kenneson and James Street sound in their book *Selling Out the Church: The Dangers of Church Marketing* is pursuing demographic groups. They feel that trying to measure target audiences is futile, largely because who are we to decide who the Holy Spirit convicts and doesn't convict? Plus, does measuring lead to marginalizing? By targeting specific demographic groups, are we marginalizing others?

These are important questions and concerns; but one thing I've learned in more than 35 years of working with churches and ministries is that each one has its own unique personality. Based on many things, such as the style of worship, the personality of the pastor, the geographic location, the denomination, each church seems to reflect the makeup of its particular congregation.

Because of those unique differences, I think it's completely appropriate for the evangelistic outreach of the church to focus first on those who might be more compatible with that church's personality. Certainly we want to welcome anyone to the service and reach out to a broad range of the public. But just as a secular business goes after the low-hanging fruit, it's perfectly appropriate for a hip, contemporary church to start with reaching out to singles; or an inner-city church to evangelize in the inner city.

That begins by knowing who you are and who you aren't. Again, defining in this way is not meant to *exclude* but to better *include*. Knowing who you aren't helps you define who you are.

6. The Sacred Words

Every great product experience comes with its own language or lingo. Where would Starbucks be without a Grande No-Foam Soy Latte, a Tall Wet Skinny Cap, or a Mocha? McDonald's has a Big Mac; Apple has an entire vocabulary of terms from iPod to iPad to iPhone; and just try to read the shorthand your teenager uses to send a text message on his or her cell phone.

Unique

Christianity has the ultimate sacred vocabulary in the Bible, and its impact on Western culture has been unprecedented. From the moment when William Tyndale began translating the Bible into English, he began to transform the language and change the world. Chuck Stetson, founder of the Bible Literacy Project in New York City, has stated that Western literature, education, art, music and more would be dramatically different without the language of the Bible. There are thousands of biblical references in Shakespeare's writings alone, and you can find biblical allusions in the greatest novels throughout history.

However, the language of Christianity is losing its currency in the world. As a result, Stetson created a foundation that published *The Bible and Its Influence*, a secondary school textbook to help public schools understand the heritage of the Bible. Without attempting to proselytize or convert, the book simply takes a student through Western history, showing him or her the myriad examples of how Judeo-Christian ideals and values have shaped the West, and the influence of the Bible through the centuries. It's a staggering project with incredible implications.

After William Tyndale translated the Bible into English, for the first time the English-speaking people had a common story. The Bible became the most widely read book in history, because it was the thread that held together the English-speaking peoples. Its publication sparked an explosion of literacy, because generations of children were taught how to read by using Bible passages and memorizing Scripture. Its influence cannot be argued. But today, that influence is waning.

When my daughters were in high school in Los Angeles, they were amazed at the number of students who had no idea what Christmas or Easter really meant, or had no concept of the Nativity or the Resurrection. These students might have been *A* students in school, but they were illiterate when it came to the Bible.

A few years ago, I saw this challenge firsthand when I went shopping in the jewelry district in downtown Los Angeles. If you want a great price on jewelry, this is the place to come. It's a multiblock area of L.A. that's filled with watch and jewelry dealers, and it's an experience all its own.

I drove down secretly one morning to look for a Christmas gift for my wife, Kathleen. As I was shopping, I began watching a young couple looking for a necklace. The dealer brought out a beautiful tray of cross necklaces ranging from simple, contemporary designs to more traditional designs featuring Jesus hanging on the cross. The young couple was very impressed, and as they looked down the row of crosses, the woman became interested in the Catholic-looking style design with the figure of Jesus on the cross.

She looked puzzled and said to the salesman, "I don't understand. Who's that little guy hanging on that cross necklace?"

She was at least 25 years old, but she had absolutely no idea who that "little guy" was or what He was doing on that necklace.

That's the culture we are trying to reach. The sacred words we use have little meaning anymore. To reach this generation, we first need to reenergize the meaning of sacred language in order to give the words value to people like that woman in the jewelry store.

7. The Leader

The last comparison point for Hanlon is the leader. In the secular world, you have to go no further than Walt Disney, Bill Gates, Steve Jobs, Jack Welch, Oprah or Thomas Edison. When it comes to values, names like Dr. Martin Luther King Jr., George Washington, Rick Warren, Mother Teresa, Bill Bright or Billy Graham appear. These are leaders that define organizations, products or ideals.

A great leader is often what causes a company to transcend the marketplace and create an emotional connection in the mind of the consumer. A recent article in *Fast Company* magazine stated, "Research suggests that brands that engage consumers emotionally can command prices as much as 20 percent to 200 percent higher than competitors' and sell in far higher volumes."[6]

Vision is what great leadership is all about; and while businesses are filled with experienced managers, most lack a strong vision to take them to the next level. As the Bible says, "Without a vision the people perish" (see Prov. 29:18).

In the Christian world, ultimate leadership and vision is found in Jesus Christ; but on the earth, we've entrusted that vision to pastors and ministry leadership. When the structure of the Early Church was set up in the New Testament, there was a need for men and women of vision, integrity and compassion. That need is still the same today.

The same holds true for nonprofit organizations. The strongest humanitarian organizations are ones that are led by visionary men and women who know how to make a connection with their donors.

> My father always said not to talk about religion, politics and money. So right here and now I'm going to break the first rule by revealing some of my most fascinating revelations by placing branding in, dare I say, a religious context.
>
> **Martin Lindstrom**
> Branding Consultant

In the entertainment world, think of the box office power of promoting a Steven Spielberg film, a Michael Bay action movie or a film by James Cameron. And look at the fiction racks at a local bookstore. In many cases, the author's name is bigger than the title of the book.

Whenever possible, I make an organization's leader an integral part of the brand, because people want to identify with a person, not a building, a program, or a radio or television show. I cannot stress enough that today's churches and nonprofits need strong leaders. Call them "servant leaders" if you like, but leaders nonetheless. Within a great brand is often a visionary leader who is able to personally identify with the purpose and reason the organization exists; and that makes a powerful connection with the audience.

Branding Revelations

While Patrick Hanlon has written the definitive book on connecting the dots between successful branding and religious belief, he's certainly not the only one crying in the wilderness. Brand futurist Martin Lindstrom has written extensively on the religious context of branding at his website at martinlindstrom.com.

Lindstrom writes that he discovered the connection between religion and branding when watching young girls on the streets of Tokyo dressed head to toe in Hello Kitty items. Apparently, nothing they carried or wore was left unbranded, even down to the Hello Kitty nails, Hello Kitty earrings and Hello Kitty cell phones. Having had two daughters who went through the Hello Kitty craze, I could relate.

This and similar observations left him wondering, "What makes people go that far? What are the ingredients that make up such an extreme brand obsession? And ultimately, what can the world of advertising learn from this when setting out to build a brand?"

After embarking on a journey to discover the ingredients that created strong religious faith, Lindstrom discovered 10 remarkable parallels between faith and branding. I like the fact that he takes great pains to indicate he doesn't believe that religious faith has actually learned anything from branding, but there's no question in his mind that branding has definitely been inspired by faith. While a few of Lindstrom's parallels are similar to Hanlon's primal branding list, I thought they were unique enough for this discussion. These could be called Martin Lindstrom's "10 Commandments of Branding."

1. A Sense of Belonging
Martin Lindstrom likes to use Weight Watchers as an example. With more than 2 million members, it's all about receiving advice and support from others in the program. The encouragement and inspiration

of peers can make a significant difference in motivation. In truth, outside of family the Church may be the original and most effective community of all. Throughout history, the Church has been involved in helping families through the most difficult aspects of life.

I was watching a movie recently that illustrated just how much the church community helps during a crisis. After a funeral service, one of the characters said, "That's what we do—after the funeral, we come over and sit. We also bring a casserole." It was a comedic line, but it made me remember all the times while I was growing up that church members would "go and sit" with people going through a crisis. A sense of belonging is critically important in a religious community, and to brands as well.

2. A Clear Vision
Lindstrom often refers to the late Steve Jobs's potent vision for Apple that began in the 1980s. A clear and powerful vision is a key part of any successful company—particularly companies that become legends. A strong vision is timeless and transcends trends, fashion and culture changes. From a religious perspective, it's not just about romantic stories such as Joan of Arc. Some of our greatest hospitals, universities and other social institutions began from a religious vision to impact the lives of people.

3. Power from the Enemy
Competition fuels global business. Coke versus Pepsi. Coors versus Budweiser. Apple versus Microsoft. Home Depot versus Lowe's. iPhone versus Android. The list is endless. In fund-raising for nonprofit or religious causes, we know that creating an enemy increases response—whether that enemy is another political party, an ideological position or a vice. The ongoing battle of sin versus salvation is the keystone of the Christian faith, and business leaders can learn much from understanding the "other."

In the arena of social media, the organization Invisible Children began by filming a documentary about Darfur in 2003, and later switched gears and went to Northern Uganda. The subsequent film—and others later—raised their profile and helped the organization grow. But it wasn't until 2012, when they released the Kony 2012 campaign focused on finding and arresting the notorius recruiter of child soldiers, Joseph Kony, that the organization exploded. Directly pointing out one evil person generated enormous media coverage, viral exposure and attention.

4. Authenticity

Lindstrom is particularly eloquent here: "Authenticity is hard to define. Are the Olympics authentic? This answer to this is unambiguously yes, because the Olympics contain the four defining components of authenticity. It's *real*, it's *relevant*, it has *rituals* and it's part of a story. More and more brands are required to be authentic—just like religion." People have always responded to faith when it seems real and relevant to their lives.

5. Consistency

In a world of constant, disruptive technological change, it's nice to feel the comfort of consistency. Throughout the ages, the religious community has been a consistent and reassuring force in the lives of people, and business brands are just beginning to notice. Whether it's the ease of ordering your coffee the exact same way at any Starbucks in the world, finding the same Big Mac or navigating your new software, people are looking for the least difficult and most familiar path. Brand consistency extends throughout the customer experience—from store design, product operation, ordering, design issues, and more. Be innovative and creative, but don't forget to be consistent.

6. Perfection

Lindstrom notes that there are as many as 521 websites dedicated solely to how to polish the engine of a Harley-Davidson. For a real fan, this attention to detail isn't an option. I have a friend who's a fanatic audiophile. The detail he looks for in a new music system is phenomenal, if not infuriating. That's why we're seeing such strong growth in "luxury" brands: high-end watches, handbags, fashion and even writing pens. People who are fans search for perfection and are willing to go to great lengths—and pay great money—to get it.

7. Symbols

Business is now global, and that means that what we encounter in the global arena needs to be as simple as possible. From airport and transportation signs, computer software, weights and measures and more, symbols are more important than ever to reach a global audience. Just like illiterate Russians used icons (biblical scenes painted on pieces of wood) to help them understand Bible stories, symbols have been pervasive throughout the history of the Church. The cross, the bread and wine, the altar, the dove are just a few of the many symbols that express different aspects of the Christian faith. Symbols help a product—just like a religious faith—to be understood in the swirl of cultural and technological change.

8. Mystery

The transcendent mystery of faith has been discussed, debated and studied since the beginning of mankind. Mystery matters, and people are endlessly fascinated with the spiritual and mysterious. In business, there are plenty of highly protected mysteries—from McDonald's secret sauce to KFC's secret spices, the Coca-Cola formula and even computer operating systems. Some are real and some are myth; but adding the element of mystery to a product or organization heightens the fun and excitement and creates a desire to explore more deeply.

9. Rituals

The power of ritual is one of the least understood aspects within the world of branding. The Catholic Church has always understood the awesome power of ritual, and I'm seeing a growing trend of Christians moving into churches today with more liturgical traditions. In the business world, I've discovered that I always get better results when I order my coffee in exactly the right sequence:

"Iced, grande, nonfat, latte." On the plane, if I order Club Soda, they always ask if I want a lime or a lemon. The Apple "bong" when a computer program starts is another example. Rituals become expected, and as such, they can become a key part of the fabric of the marketing experience.

10. Sensory Appeal

In liturgical churches, they sometimes refer to this as the "smells and bells." For thousands of years, religious communities have understood the power of engaging a worshiper's sense of smell, sound, sight and taste. It creates the sense that you're in another world and lifts you into a more focused worship experience. As Lindstrom noted, the rise in "flagship" stores for companies such as Nike, Disney or Apple help a customer move from the everyday world into a new brand experience. Stores like Victoria's Secret or Bath and Body Works further enhance the experience with smells. The background music is also highly researched in an attempt to soothe and motivate the customer but not distract him or her from the buying experience. It's about intensifying the sensations around the product and creating a unique sensory encounter. So the next time you walk into an Anthropologie store, remember that they're taking their cues from thousands of years of Church history.[7]

Is Branding a Religion?

In Lindstrom's words, "Whether we love it or hate it, the world of branding is becoming increasingly inspired by the world of religion. Religion offers a powerful roadmap for how branding can evolve over the years to come. All it needs to do is look to the ancient ingredients that make up religious followings. In some cases this is so powerful that the brand becomes more than a brand, and it becomes a way of life."[8]

When I first encountered the writings of Patrick Hanlon and Martin Lindstrom, I realized that Christians should have known this all along. The story of the Christian faith is filled with all the elements that connect with a person, offer conviction and cause a change in his or her heart and life. Ultimately, Christianity is about change. Although "conversion" has become a bad word in this supposedly "tolerant" society, the truth is, "conversion" and "repenting" mean that you change your thinking.

The Holy Spirit has been helping people do that for centuries and, finally, the marketing world has discovered its impact.

Take Your **Thinking Deeper**

1. How do you see popular brands tap into our collective need for community and our desire to be part of a group?

2. How do you see a connection between branding and relationships?

3. Based on the information in this chapter, is your organization's story expressing real meaning? Is it answering significant questions this culture—especially your audience or customer—is asking?

4. Think more about how the apostle Paul, in Acts 17, connected with that culture. What were the techniques he used, and how could you adapt those techniques to your immediate situation?

5. In studying Martin Lindstrom's list from his book *Primal Branding*, how many of these should be considered in your own efforts to connect with your potential audience? What are things you can do right now to use these ideas in your marketing and promotional efforts?

Telling Your Story

> Show me a successful business, and I'll
> show you a triumph of storytelling.
> **Leonard Sweet**
> Social Critic and Writer

> There's something evangelistic
> about what we do.
> **Lloyd Hill**
> CEO, Applebee's Restaurants

FedEx, eBay, McDonalds, Mercedes, Shell. All it takes is a logo, and you know the exact company represented and what the logo means. Not long ago, I was driving in St. Louis and saw a white roadside billboard with nothing on it but the Nike swoosh. No letters, no pictures, just the swoosh icon. (Interesting that it's called an "icon.") At that moment, I realized that the vast majority of people who drive past that billboard know exactly what company is represented and the meaning of the symbol. At the same time, the phrase "Just Do It" probably races through their minds. That's the power of a compelling brand.

What if your church or nonprofit organization had that same kind of visual recognition in your community? What if your story, purpose and meaning were so clear that all it took was a simple graphic design to remind people about you and your message?

Some simple searching on the Internet reveals the focus of Nike's brand:

The spirit of the athlete.

It doesn't say anything about shoes, quality or price, and yet it expresses the company and its vision perfectly. Everything Nike does is caught up in that simple phrase.

Notice, by the way, that the statement isn't the phrase "Just Do It." That's a *tagline*. A tagline is a public statement that expresses the brand through advertising and promotion. A brand focus or statement is normally for insiders—people inside the company—to help them understand the identity you've created.

Taglines can be used for individual advertising campaigns and can change as advertising and marketing concepts change. These slogans are more flexible and can be very effective.

Some of the earliest advertising slogans can be traced to the late 1890s when business leaders realized the power of emotion to sell products. The website taglineguru.com keeps a listing of the "100 Most Influential Taglines Since 1948." It's a fascinating list, and I would encourage you to check it out. Here are the top 10 on the list:

1. Got milk? (1993, California Milk Processor Board)
2. Don't leave home without it. (1975, American Express)
3. Just do it. (1988, Nike)
4. Where's the beef? (1984, Wendy's)
5. You're in good hands with Allstate. (1956, Allstate Insurance)
6. Think different. (1998, Apple Computer)
7. We try harder. (1962, Avis)
8. Tastes great, less filling. (1974, Miller Lite)
9. Melts in your mouth, not in your hand. (1954, M&M Candies)
10. Takes a licking and keeps on ticking. (1956, Timex)

A brand statement, on the other hand, is an overall identity for the company. Here is Starbucks's brand focus:

A great coffee experience.

That statement means so much more than just a good cup of coffee. It resonates throughout the design of the store, the menu selections, the attitude of the employees, the multiple locations, the consistency of the product, and more. I have no idea if it's true, but not long ago, I heard a story that a hotshot MBA came into the company and decided to do some cost cutting. I'm told he did a sheet by sheet, roll by roll, store by store study of toilet paper used at the coffee shops and discovered that by changing from two-ply toilet paper to one-ply, he could save the company hundreds of thousands of dollars.

After a major meeting, it was decided that Starbucks would continue to spend the extra money and supply their restrooms with two-ply paper. It was apparently decided that single-ply toilet paper doesn't make for "A Great Coffee Experience."

I'm sure you would agree.

True, or not? I don't know, but it's a perfect example of how the brand focus should permeate every aspect of the organization, ministry or nonprofit. It's not just about the "product"; it's about all the things that happen when a customer comes in contact with your product or company.

Now let's look at how that thinking can impact your particular brand.

Understanding Who You Are

Whenever my company brands a nonprofit and ministry client, we take them through an extensive branding and identity process that helps us determine their brand story. We ask these questions: What is the ultimate expression of the particular church, ministry, pastor or spiritual leader? As a nonprofit, what's your ultimate expression of mission? What are you here to accomplish? What is the brand story you want to communicate to your congregation, donors, television viewers, online audience, readers or customers? What is their current perception of you or your organization?

In other words, *What do they think of when they think of you?*

In these sessions, we always want to be sensitive and compassionate. Successful ministry in the twenty-first century is a complex enterprise; and in a postmodern culture, a thriving outreach is contingent on a number of issues, not the least of which is the grace of God.

I obviously have no control over the client's personal calling or relationship with God. So we concentrate on the aspects we *can* control and focus on the issues that tell the story most effectively. Our purpose is to discover the story or identity that makes the client different and sets the organization apart.

I'd like to help you do the same. So, if terms like "marketing" or "branding" are still uncomfortable for you, I would encourage you to read on and give it a little time. But from this point on, I'll assume that we're on the same page, and our goal is to determine how to tell the most effective story about who you are; what your idea, business or ministry is about; and how that vision can impact people's lives.

The Branding Focus

In the religious or nonprofit world, when I work with a particular pastor or ministry leader, it's usually in the context of a media outreach. Our company, Cooke Pictures (cookepictures.com), produces programming and consults with some of the largest churches and ministries in the country on how to improve their effectiveness in the media. The consultation could be a project with television, radio, a website, print or social media, or other emerging platforms. Our passion is reaching an audience, and we're usually called in when a media ministry has hit a plateau or is having difficulty reaching the next level.

In many cases, we choose to focus much of our efforts on the pastor or ministry leader, not just the church or ministry itself. If your church is in Dallas, and your market is local, then you can focus your marketing efforts on how your *church* impacts that city. But with a national or international outreach—particularly through media— your viewers or listeners outside Dallas—in places like Los Angeles or Miami—will probably never visit your church; they're interested in what they see on television, short films, on the Web or podcasts, hear on radio, engage through social media, or read in your books. Perhaps they'll listen to your message streamed online. Especially when it comes to preaching and teaching ministries, in most cases we've discovered that people tune in to hear the pastor's teaching; so, in branding a national media ministry, we usually focus on the personality that leads that ministry.

The Cultural Reality of Celebrity

Today, some national ministry leaders have become "stars" to the point that they're forced to fly in private jets because they get mobbed at airports. I saw one very vocal woman grab a well-known pastor by the arm in the produce section of a grocery store and loudly beg for his autograph. It was humiliating for the pastor and his family, not to mention just plain strange for the other shoppers. While most people criticize these leaders, it's the general public that has created the phenomenon. Much like entertainment celebrities in Hollywood, the Christian community has bought into the concept of celebrity in a big way.

I was in a meeting recently with a major ministry figure who happens to be a best-selling author. He's so successful in selling books that the publisher was pushing him to create a series of novels. This particular ministry leader doesn't read novels, doesn't care for novels and has no desire to write a novel. But his readership is so loyal that they would buy anything with his name on it.

So they decided to look for fictional storylines, hire a ghost-writer (a professional writer who writes books for other people), and then have the ministry leader put his name on the finished novel. I'm sure the sales will go through the roof.

This is the dark side of branding. It's done all the time in the secular world. (Do you *really* think most professional athletes, politicians or movie stars write well?) But when it happens in the religious world, it's a little disconcerting, to say the least.

Don't Throw the Baby Out with the Bathwater

I passionately believe in branding, but it can be abused. At my online blog at philcooke.com, these conversations happen on a regular basis, and the debate and discussions often get pretty passionate in both directions. But just as we don't stop taking an offering at church because some pastors take financial advantage of people, neither do we dump marketing and branding because some choose to use it for manipulation.

Christian celebrity is a fact of life, and we can't control that. So we need to move beyond it to understand the *purpose* of branding and marketing. I choose to brand *a pastor or ministry leader* in most cases, particularly when the goal is to create a national media outreach. I tend to brand the pastor or ministry leader to some degree even when marketing on the local level. In a perfect world, people would come to your church for a multitude of reasons—children's ministry, youth programs, missions, worship, community. But in reality, most people first experience a church because of what they hear in the pulpit.

If your church or ministry is in Atlanta, people in Des Moines, Tulsa or Birmingham will probably never come to your church; so focusing on the music, worship or community will mean very little to them. They're usually looking for your personal ministry, and that's why we focus on you. Examples of compelling personal ministries might be pastors like Greg Laurie, Joel Osteen, Benny Perez, Charles Jenkins, David McGee, Mark Jeske, Craig Groeschel, James McDonald, Kyle Searcy, Erwin McManus, Jack Graham, Gary Keesee, or John MacArthur. All of these leaders have vibrant local churches, but viewers or listeners *outside* their geographical area are more interested in their personal teaching or preaching ministries through print, TV, radio or online.

Recently, I visited a church that was voting on calling a new pastor. The church board was supporting a candidate who was highly organized, a great manager and was excellent with people. He had long experience as an administrator, and from that perspective, he was an excellent choice. The only sticky problem was that he was completely inept in the pulpit. His sermons were dry, he couldn't tell stories well and he was embarrassed and awkward on the platform. It was so bad that even loyal members of the congregation were visibly uncomfortable watching him preach.

The board, being concerned about the whole picture, was more than willing to overlook his lack of skill in the pulpit and focus on his abilities managing the church. In a perfect world, that might work. Certainly there are many things that contribute to the worship experience, and the 40-minute message on Sunday shouldn't overpower all the other gifts and talents in a pastor's arsenal.

But I felt compelled to remind them that if church growth was a concern, they should rethink their direction. After all, our experience indicates that the Sunday morning service is the main entry portal for the vast majority of people who visit. Who wants to bring a friend to hear a pastor who can't preach? The 40-minute message on Sunday morning may seem like a small part of the overall experience, but in most cases, it's the pastor in the pulpit who casts the vision for the church, motivates the congregation and inspires growth.

This church didn't take my advice, and since that time, the church has been wonderfully managed but attendance has dramatically declined.

I met another pastor who was a wonderful man, but he was one of the worst preachers I've ever met. He loved God and was great with people, but he was simply a catastrophe in the pulpit. As a result, he had been the pastor of 18 churches in his 21 years of ministry. He kept getting asked to leave because he simply couldn't preach. I was fascinated to find out how long it would take him to realize that perhaps preaching was not his gift.

This book isn't about bad preaching. My point is that while at the local level there are certainly different points of view and various possibilities for branding, one thing I've discovered is that the pastor or ministry leader is the hub of the brand. Everything else revolves around his or her role.

The digital culture has dramatically changed how we communicate.

I may take some flak for that thinking, and to be honest, I personally don't like it either. But that's another example of the changes we need to make to reach an audience in a media-driven world. We first must understand how people initially connect and then develop our branding and identity from there.

Another important reason the pastor or ministry leader is a critical key to branding is that in the media, people ultimately want a relationship with a person—not a program, a building or a ministry. This is one of the key reasons for the explosion of social media. So in order to develop fund-raising, partnership or mission, focusing on the leader is key.

Personal Branding

We call this technique "personal branding." In my book *One Big Thing: Discovering What You Were Born to Do,* I use examples from the excellent book *The Brand Called You* by Peter Montoya. The examples are worth revisiting here. In his book, Montoya shares three critical insights for creating a compelling personal brand.[1]

1. Visibility Is Just as Important as Ability
In a media-driven culture, being seen is just as important as being effective. There are hundreds of brilliant, gifted pastors who will never make an impact because people don't know who they are. You see the concept illustrated most clearly in Hollywood, where actors of little ability and skill make millions of dollars from be-

ing in the right place at the right time. As a producer and director, I'm amazed at the incredible level of talent among unknown actors I see in casting sessions. There are men and women with incredible gifts who will never be recognized or known, simply because they don't know how to get noticed.

In ministry, the people you see on television or listen to on radio aren't necessarily the most gifted, anointed or skilled ministry leaders out there. But they have influence because they have visibility.

Does ability matter? No question about it. I believe in education, skill, expertise and personal growth. When the door opens, you'd better be ready to act and have the talent and calling to back it up. But unless that door opens, all the talent in the world will do little outside of entertaining your family. I don't care how great your sermon, screenplay, movie or business idea may be. If it can't get in front of the right people, you've failed.

Getting your face out there isn't necessarily the act of an egotistical maniac. Certainly there are narcissists in the media (and plenty in religious media), but the truth is, getting on the radar of the public is the first step toward getting your message heard.

2. You Can't Brand a Lie

Certainly, as people of faith, we should act with integrity; and every expression of your ministry should be true. But when it comes to skill and expertise, I find that a great number of ministry leaders take a shortcut. Through advertising and promotion, pastors often indicate areas of expertise they don't really have, or experience that's never actually happened.

Just check out the advertisements for the latest Christian conferences and look for the number of "Dr." degrees. Everybody in ministry is a Doctor of something these days. And don't get me started on the number of "Bishops," "Prophets," "Prophetesses," "Apostles," and more. Some denominations continue to use some of these designations in official ministry capacities, but many simply make it up to sound good.

When the truth is revealed, false branding dies hard. Montoya cites the case of television evangelist Jimmy Swaggart:

> A perfect example is Jimmy Swaggart, the television minister who waged war on evil until he publicly admitted to an unspecified "sin" that later turned out to be cavorting with prostitutes. Despite his famous, tearful "I have sinned against you" speech, and his penitence, Swaggart has never rehabilitated his image because so many of his followers felt extremely and irreversibly betrayed.[2]

I don't use that example to criticize Jimmy Swaggart or comment on his sincerity, or his relationship with God. I use the quote as a powerfully clear example of the damage caused when brands are betrayed.

Keep in mind that perception plays a significant role in the process. In 2006, when pastor Ted Haggard resigned from his church in Colorado Springs under a cloud of alleged sexual misconduct, there were multiple issues at play, including how poorly he and his staff handled the media. I'll never forget watching the news broadcast when they featured an interview with Ted after he stopped his car at the end of the driveway with his wife and kids in the backseat. An impromptu interview in the front yard in earshot of the kids wasn't the most appropriate venue to answer questions about alleged sexual wrongdoing.

Who can possibly know how difficult struggling with this issue for years had been, and how humiliating the experience was for Ted and his family. We all struggle with sin in our lives, and it's important to remind ourselves just how easy it is to stumble or fall.

This discussion is not meant to be a personal criticism of anyone. But for the Church as a whole, we need to wake up to living and sharing our witness in a media-saturated culture. The way the mass media exposes, uncovers and tells the story is vastly different from anything the Church has experienced in 2,000 years of its history. If we don't understand how the media works, it will forever damage our witness to the world.

And it's not about covering up, deflecting or denying. On the contrary, it's about being truthful and confronting the media in a way that permits the real story to be told without letting denials, information scraps, inaccuracies and falsehoods color the story. The stakes are remarkably high. At the time, it didn't take much to see the anti-religious bloggers and writers descending on the Haggard story like sharks to blood.

> ## With any crisis in the Church today, hypocrisy, denials or botched public statements energize Christianity's critics.

In fact, it was sobering to note an America Online poll that asked 185,364 people what they thought of Ted's confession. In my opinion, largely because of the poor handling of the story, 65 percent of the respondents said they believed his confession was insincere, and only 35 percent felt it was sincere.[3]

During the weeks after the story broke, "Ted Haggard" was the most searched name on multiple search engines, and Technorati. com revealed that it was the number-one topic among bloggers. That means that in spite of the war in Iraq, and on the eve of a national mid-term election, this was the number-one priority for the American people. Millions of people were asking about it, searching for information and writing about the issue. But the Sunday morning after the story broke, I attended a church here in Los Angeles and then asked my friends about their own churches, and not one pastor even mentioned it. Not once. It was the most asked question on people's minds in the country, and these—and thousands of other—pastors chose not to engage in a conversation about sin, denial, forgiveness, restoration and salvation—or even offer to pray for Ted and his family. What a missed opportunity!

When it comes to branding a lie, it's also not simply about moral failure; it's about gifts, talents and expertise. If you bill yourself as an expert on drug treatment, you'd better be able to back it up. If you want to become known for family ministry, you'd better have the credentials to prove it. If you write or teach on financial success, you'd better have some money in the bank.

> This is why so many in the culture think the
> church is irrelevant. The world is asking questions,
> but we refuse to deal with them.

In this age of the Internet, anyone can be investigated, any time, with a few easy keystrokes on a computer. Politicians are finding this out in the heat of campaigns, as old DUI convictions suddenly pop up, a racist remark is uncovered, or embarrassing academic records are revealed. (Can you say, "mail-order Ph.D."?) Major corporations struggle as confidential internal memos are released on the Internet as quickly as they're distributed to employees.

> Never in history have leaders needed to
> be more transparent.

We live in a world of video cameras, databases and information retrieval. In fact, search engines aren't just about "search"; they're about "reputation management." For a generation of young people who grew up posting the most intimate details of their lives on social media sites, they're finding in their twenties that it's getting tough to find a job. Once the interview is complete, the first thing a future employer often does is Google them, only to find the old drinking photos from the college dorm, a raging political rant, embarrassing personal details, explicit sexual updates, and more.

Hardly welcome news for a prospective employer.

In the old days, executives, pastors and nonprofit leaders could have a private jet, a luxury car or a mansion, and few would ever find out. But today, a few keystrokes on the computer reveal everything.

3. In a Media-driven Culture, Being Different Is Everything

The world isn't looking for a copy of a major religious leader; they are looking for someone new, innovative and original. God gave you unique DNA, so your job is to discover how your unique gifts and talents can differentiate your ministry from everyone else's.

Differentiate or die.
Jack Trout
Marketing Consultant

You have no idea the number of pastors who call our offices each week asking us to "Do the same thing for us that you did for this or that national ministry client." They've got it backward. There's already one of *them*. You need to emphasize your unique *differences*.

In working with these pastors and ministry leaders, I'm reminded of Michelangelo, who was asked about how he carved such brilliant statues of angels. He remarked that he didn't carve statues; he just removed the excess stone so that the angel inside could come out.

> It's not so much a matter of re-creating or rebuilding a ministry; it's more about cutting away the junk so that the real ministry that's inside can be released.

And believe me, the junk is there. Lack of professionalism, poor media production, unqualified staff, poor taste, inept leadership, insecurity, small budgets, bad assumptions and more plague many organizations today and hamper their effectiveness.

A quick look at Christian television will prove that most ministries are pretty similar in their look, style and presentation. Few men and women in the ministry world are truly unique. God is the great creator, and yet most ministry leaders simply copy what they see on TV or hear on the radio.

Listen to Apple ads and "Think Different." If God created you as a unique individual, what does that mean for the type of vision you're called to accomplish?

The Branding Team

While we do focus groups with various stakeholders in an organization, when my team brands a product, person or organization, we usually have a special session with people closest to the client (pastor, ministry, business or nonprofit leader). This often includes the spouse and, sometimes, grown or particularly mature children, especially if they work in the ministry. (After all, they've seen the organization from the inside.) Then we ask that key members of the leadership team be present. These staff members are especially important to the process if they know the client closely and have experienced a long working relationship.

While our branding sessions cover many days and dig deep into the nature of the organization, there are four key questions we always ask. Let's walk through these questions in light of your own personal and organizational brand:

Branding Question #1: What's the Point?
When I help a client with branding, I usually begin with a question the secular world of branding doesn't ask (or rarely asks). That question is, *What's the point?* or, *Why are you doing this?* When branding a hammer, a cold medication, a computer or other product, the *motivation* of the company doesn't mean nearly as much as when branding a church, ministry or nonprofit. With some variation, most consultants in the secular advertising and marketing world refer to a "branding triangle," featuring three questions:

1. Who are you?
2. What are your gifts and talents?
3. What makes you unique and different?

I use these questions as well, but I prefer to begin with a different question that revolves around the person's calling, passion, motivation and the driving force behind the mission he or she is trying to accomplish. A conversion experience and subsequent ministry calling are certainly important to this question, but the answer usually lies in another area.

For instance, just this morning, I was watching writer and teacher Beth Moore on television. During the program, she talked about her experience as a victim of childhood abuse. She mentioned the encounter as the focal point that drives her ministry today—to the point that not a single day goes by when that incident doesn't come into play somehow in her ministry.

She can understand other victims of abuse because she's been there and understands their pain. Her own experience keeps her from becoming prideful. It helps her minister more effectively because of the way God helped her through the devastating trauma. She went on to say how her past has helped her understand the providence of God, because although God didn't cause the abuse, He's been able to use the experience to make her ministry more effective to millions of women.

She's a best-selling writer, a brilliant speaker and a strong Bible teacher. But her childhood abuse is a key part of what drives Beth Moore.

Franklin Graham's struggle growing up with a famous ministry father was a key part of the journey to becoming an evangelist himself. Nancy Alcorn's frustration at the neglect and hurtful treatment of pregnant single women drove her to build a global network of Mercy Ministry homes that counsel, teach and train young mothers.

Many social activists work from a past that motivates them toward change. Some leaders are particularly focused on ministry to businesspeople because they came out of that background. Many pastors were driven in their younger years by sports.

With some people, their motivation is trauma; with others, it's triumph.

Pastor, leader, filmmaker, musician, writer, actor, entrepreneur—what's the point? What drives you? Is there a consuming fire that burns within your heart? Is there a desire that can't be quenched? Your passion might be the result of your background, either as a child or an adult; it might be a particular expertise in an unusual area; it might be something you've felt strongly about all your life.

> If you are here to be an artist,
> Hollywood will not stop you.
> If you are here to be a celebrity,
> Hollywood will kill you.
>
> **Jim Covell**
> Film Composer

Whatever your driving motivation, it will impact the brand story about you and your project, business or ministry. The fact that the pastor of an outreach to bikers was a member of an outlaw motorcycle gang before he became a Christian is a key element in presenting his identity. A career geneticist might begin a nonprofit focused on resolving issues of faith and science. A businessman who is fascinated by a particular area of study might begin a foundation that funds educational programs for decades to come. If you want to minister to Hollywood professionals, although it's not required, a credible career of your own as an actor, producer or other media role is significantly helpful to engage your audience.

There are actually two issues at stake here: *credibility* and *motive*.

Credibility. If you have experience in a particular area, it becomes far easier to win support from your potential audience. If you have a passion for sports, movies, church history or psychology, that passion should figure into your branding in some unique way. In the same vein, past trauma might be helpful in ministry to others who have experienced similar struggles. Having a medical background gives you credibility in raising money for a medical outreach to the Third World.

Building your brand story often begins with your past and your purpose.

Motive. I've discovered that a successful and fulfilling life in the nonprofit world comes from years of difficult work—plowing new ground and pioneering where others often fear to tread. During the difficult times, your motive will be a key driving force to keep your momentum moving forward. If Beth Moore's motivation was to be a celebrity, chances are, all the frustrating years she studied and worked in oblivion would have caused her to give up. But because she's driven by her experience of abuse and the potential to help others get through their own trauma, she has the determination to keep going.

Embrace your past. One of the reasons I bring up this issue is that staggering numbers of pastors and ministry leaders run away from their past. They make no connection with an experience or an expertise that could help fuel their ministry and provide great credibility with their audience.

In recent years, pastors and ministry leaders have been less afraid to admit past struggles and mistakes, and they've discovered that it often actually strengthens the bond with their partners and supporters.

And by the way, when it comes to your point, I'm not interested in big-picture answers like "I want to reach the nations with the gospel" or "I want to start a billion-dollar company."

Duh. Everyone wants to do that. The question is, what *specific and personal* reason drives you? Narrow it down.

So ask yourself again: *Why am I doing this?* Figure it out, and it will help you discover your brand story.

Branding Question #2: Who Are You?

The second question is, *Who exactly are you?* The purpose of this question is to discover what makes you who you are. Do you come from a rich or poor family? Are you an immigrant? Do you have less than a high school education? Do you have a college education or graduate degree? Are you from a distinctive geographic region such as the South? Married or single? Fat or skinny? Handicapped? Tall or short? Conservative or liberal? Do you suffer from Attention Deficit Disorder? The questions could go on, but you get the idea.

Your goal is to discover your unique DNA, or how you're personally wired. A pastor with a thick Southern accent who was raised by cotton farmers is going to have a different perspective on life than a rich prep-school grad from New England. An evangelist who cut his teeth on inner-city ministry will be different than a rural tent revivalist. A leader with an academic focus will view life differently from a pastor with a street ministry to addicts. A businessman who builds a museum will have a different perspective from a Ph.D. who does the same thing.

This is critical information even in today's culture of absorption. If you really delve into your past—your family history and your upbringing—it will reveal a lot about who you are and how you function today. Do you have unresolved issues with your father or mother? If you were abused or abandoned as a child and have never adequately dealt with it, sooner or later it will come up.

A saved turkey is still a turkey.

In spite of God's saving grace, and even after you've made Jesus Christ the Lord of your life, you often carry baggage from your past. Saved or not, childhood abuse doesn't go away; hurt and pain don't necessarily disappear; and your educational or financial limitations are still present. Certainly you have a new resource to deal with those issues, and the power of God in your life can transform your circumstances, but salvation isn't necessarily about making obstacles disappear.

We preach from the pulpit a message about the need for continued growth in our Christian walk, but we often don't deal with it in our own lives. That's why, when I'm helping to position a client in the most effective way possible, it's critically important to discover his or her personal issues, both positive and negative.

I wrestle a great deal with how ministry leaders are wired. Certainly, God can heal any weakness or negative personality trait; but I've discovered that most people carry deep-seated issues throughout their life. In those cases, we have to learn to work within those limitations or, better yet, use them to our advantage.

How My Weakness Has Become an Advantage

Most people who know me would agree that I'm the king of the short attention span. For years, when people would come into my office for a meeting, my assistant would whisper in their ear, "When his eyes glaze over, the meeting is finished."

In my case, it's about *distraction*. As long as I can remember, I could be distracted by anything, any time. As a preacher's kid who had to sit on the front row every time the church doors were open, I knew the exact number of ceiling tiles in the sanctuary and the number of steps across the stage, and I had mentally traced every design on the altar a million times. As my dad preached, my mind raced; and it still races today.

As a result, I have to close the shutters on my office windows when I write, and I have to turn off my email or else those little messages start calling my name. I've discovered that I'm most productive when I'm trapped. So I always take my laptop on planes, where my distractions are limited and my options are few.

In spite of those frustrations and limitations, I've learned to channel my personality in positive directions. I've discovered I'm interested in a wide variety of pursuits: I produce media programming; consult with clients; have a regular speaking schedule; and I write numerous magazine articles, books and my personal blog.

It might be why I gravitated to being a multicamera television director. During a show, I can talk to 10 or more camera operators, the sound and lighting crew, the video guy, technical director, producer and probably a few more—and for me, that seems perfectly normal.

I've learned to take what most people would consider a negative and turn it into a positive.

Life can throw us a lot of curves.

In consultation meetings with a client pastor or ministry leader, we've discovered insights that surprised the client and helped us enormously in our branding work with them. For instance, one pastor who is considered highly experienced and has a very successful television program discovered from his team that his church members considered him aloof, distant and cold. It wasn't behavior he intentionally modeled, but because of the size of his church and the scope of his ministry, cultivating personal relationships was difficult for him. It had become obvious to the people that surrounded him, but not to the pastor. Dealing with 8 people when starting a church in a living room is radically different from growing to 8,000 in an arena-sized sanctuary.

In another case, we discovered a CEO who was so detail-oriented that he was approving light bulb purchases for the company in spite of the fact that he had more than 100 employees. I gently reminded him that his job was to lead, not get bogged down in the day-to-day operations of the ministry.

Others have discovered that their regional accent was so strong that they were difficult to understand in the pulpit, or their choice in clothes made people uncomfortable, or their attitude made it difficult to relate to their own employees. Were these issues obvious? Not to the pastor or executive. Were they important for the organization? Absolutely. Anything that hinders or frustrates the full operation of your gifts and talents is something that should be dealt with as soon as possible.

The Big Picture of How You're Wired
We've spent some time defining negative traits that impact branding. Positive character and personality traits are also a crit-

ical part of defining a successful brand. Here are both positive and negative possibilities you might list about yourself as you work on defining your brand:

Enthusiastic	Conservative
Controlling	Liberal
Passive	Modest
Loyal	Withdrawn
Systematic	Change-oriented
Perfectionist	Deliberate
Mature	Firm
Sensitive	Opinionated
Visionary	Tactless
Charismatic	Creative
Outgoing	Quality-driven
People-oriented	Obsessive
Patient	Critical
Passionate	Educated
Fun	Timid
Decisive	Sarcastic
Retrained	Witty

Consider all the personal qualities that make you human and add them to this list. The question "Who are you?" becomes a vital foundation stone for knowing what you're made of. And don't be so sure that you know all the answers until you get your team in the room with you.

This kind of assessment is similar to professional personality tests available today through psychologists, counselors and business consultants. I would encourage you to explore these types of assessments and other possibilities in a biblically responsible manner. I'm for any proven tool that helps you see an objective view of your strengths and weaknesses, because without an adequate assessment, you'll never discover your true potential.

Branding Question #3: What Are Your Gifts and Talents?
The third question discovers the areas where you really excel. The key to answering this question is brutal honesty. The question is not "What would you *like* to be good at doing in the future?" It's "What are you good (or gifted) at *now*?" I always recommend a "come to Jesus" meeting with yourself on this one, and if you're working with your team, make sure they are absolutely honest with you.

Here are some of the answers I've received from clients who have described their gifts and talents:

Preaching	Fund-raising
Teaching	Administration
Writing	Team building
Leading	Financial management
Managing	Media ministry
Singing	Intercessory prayer
Leading worship	Music
Technology	Sports
Education	Development
Business	Fitness
Youth ministry	Construction
Missions	

There are many more options, and the list can be a long one, depending on the particular gifts and talents you may have.

This is where we find out if what you're doing matches your skill set. If you're the senior pastor, but you can't preach, there might be a problem. If you're a youth director, but you hate working with kids, we should rethink your future. If you're a CEO and don't understand finances, we have a challenge.

In most cases, it's not so obvious as those examples. In one case, a leader started out in evangelistic ministry only to encounter serious challenges with fund-raising, managing a ministry, working with a team, and more. Once we explored his personal gifts in relation to the brand, we realized that he was better suited as a writer. In that capacity he didn't have to raise money, manage a team or worry about invitations to preach. Once he left traditional evangelism and focused on writing books, his ministry blossomed.

In another case, a young couple in youth ministry in Los Angeles were miserable. They loved young people but they just didn't seem suited for the job. I offered to explore their brand through questions like the ones we've just discussed. We discovered they were actually wired for missions. Today they manage a growing Christian school in Mexico.

> Traditionally in the Church, we've rightly put enormous emphasis on calling but haven't spent much time connecting that calling to actual gifts and talents.

Today, we have far too many pastors who shouldn't be in the pulpit; youth leaders that teenagers can't relate to; missionaries who are ill-equipped and miserable. Some organizations have developed personal gift inventories and evaluations, and I applaud those resources. They can be exceptional tools for helping believers truly understand how their abilities and spiritual gifts impact their calling. Personality profiles are also helpful resources for revealing personal strengths and weaknesses.

There's no question that God can transcend personal gifts and talents, and He does so on occasion. Sometimes we need to be put in a position where it's clear that our personal abilities cannot accomplish our goal and we need to rely on God's power and grace. Nehemiah rebuilt the walls of Jerusalem while facing enormous opposition, and yet he knew nothing about fortress design and construction. He was a cupbearer to the king and spent his life doing little more than working in the kitchen. If he had any skill at all, he was probably an expert on wine. But he had a willing heart and was open to learning and to the power of change. In the face of criticism, apathy and threats on his life, he rallied the

Jewish people and accomplished something that gave an entire nation hope.

Never close the door on the possibilities God can accomplish through your life with or without the appropriate skill set. But your job isn't to take the easy way out. You can't sit on the sofa and wait for God when you should be learning, growing and developing your gifts and talents.

Someone once said that if you make stoves, you should be famous among cooks. If you make fishing lures, you should be famous among fishermen. And if you make airplanes, you should be famous among pilots. You can't be all things to all people when it comes to marketing. What do your specific gifts and talents say about the potential audience that could benefit from your particular ministry?

Your real gifts and talents may have nothing to do with your present position.

Forbid the thought, but just because you're a pastor right now doesn't necessarily mean that you have a talent or calling for that job. You may be leading a church, managing a nonprofit, or running a Christian television studio or network; but perhaps you got the job based on something other than your skill. Although usually motivated by good intentions, family connections have often driven people into jobs and careers that ruined their lives. Never be deluded into thinking that being in your present job means that you're actually qualified for it.

One of the most tragic situations I encounter is when a famous ministry parent pushes his or her son or daughter into the same calling without taking the time to explore the son's or daughter's unique gifts and talents. In some cases, the parent is driven by such ego that he or she would never consider another alternative; but for most, it's a financial consideration: The church or ministry has simply grown so large that the founder feels that a "successor" is the only way to continue the legacy.

I've seen ministries in which a son felt the burden so powerfully that he completely sublimated his own dreams to copy the ministry of his famous father. As a result, he never discovered his own story or "brand"; once the father and his financial supporters eventually died, the son had to start building his own unique identity, but by then it was too late.

That's why this branding exercise is so critically important. Our goal is to motivate you to find the right expression for your gifts and talents. You may have been born to write or you learned to preach in school or you inherited an uncanny ability to relate to others. Whatever your gifts and talents, identifying them accurately can save you from a life of frustration and failure.

Branding Question #4: What Makes You Different?

Finally, you need to discover what separates you from the pack. In the secular advertising world, this is sometimes referred to as "the unique selling proposition." In other words, what's different and unique about your product compared to the competition?

In a media-driven world, being different is everything. Near the turn of the century, my grandmother's family shopped at a rural grocery store in North Carolina, and choices weren't part of the process. They found one brand of flour, one type of butter and one source of milk.

Today, when my wife, Kathleen, shops at the local grocery store, she faces thousands of choices. On my last visit, I noticed about 12 types of Oreo cookies. Even staples like butter, milk, sugar and flour compete for consumers' favor by offering almost endless variations, such as low-fat, skim, flavored, sugar-free, almond, soy, and so on. Butter and milk can even come from a wide variety of animals and feature a wide variety of flavors.

Bottled water is one of my favorite branding examples. When I was growing up, I always thought water was free (stupid me). But in bottled form, it's not only expensive (bought in bulk it's more expensive than gasoline), but you also can find a wide range of varieties. The question is, outside the obvious choice of flavored, vitamin-enriched or energy-laden water, what's the big difference?

It's *branding*. Sure, there may be slight variations in taste because different companies bottle water from different sources. But the real difference is *perception*. It's not a *content* issue; it's a *style* issue.

It's about the branding.

It's not about the water; it's about the story told by the bottle. Their advertising continues that story of "cool" and "sophistication" so that it connects with the customer.

> ## With bottled water, it's not about the content; it's about the branding.

In the same way, there are a massive number of churches in your city, a multitude of ministries and nonprofits, and a host of preachers and ministry leaders.

Publishers receive thousands of book manuscripts from hopeful writers.

Studios are mailed a mountain of screenplays and grow deaf from endless movie pitches.

Investors are flooded with funding requests.

What makes you different?

Beyond the other churches and ministries, there's even more competition out there within the greater culture. How can you compete with all the entertainment choices, lifestyle options or new digital technologies that struggle to engage the average person's limited discretionary time? You may not have the resources, finances or assets of the competition, but you can tell a better story; and the key to finding that story is discovering what makes you unique and different.

Perhaps it's your unique preaching or teaching style, your writing ability, your personality, or an expertise in an unusual area. Being different can mean many things, including perspective, content, skill and delivery.

Perhaps your humanitarian organization does the same thing—say, feeding the hungry—as many other organizations, but you need to find a different way of doing it or do it in a different place. In the pursuit of support and donor dollars, something needs to make your work stand out.

If your focus is the media, think of an area that isn't covered right now on radio or television. When James Dobson began his radio program many years ago, there weren't many programs talking about parenting and family issues. The same was true of other ministries that focused around finances, prophecy or marketplace ministry. It's about pushing creativity to its limits and discovering what it's like to explore life from the perspective of a Bible that starts with "In the beginning, God *created*."

Branding the Real Thing

Ultimately, successful branding is all about authenticity because being unique and different doesn't mean fake. Someone once said that *Hollywood does an incredible job of making fake things look real, and Christians do an incredible job of making real things look fake.* In our efforts to relate to the culture, churches and ministries often go over the top and end up conveying a message that's obviously dishonest and far from authentic.

I'm told that I was born with the gift of saying what everyone else in the room is thinking. Whether or not it gets me in trouble, I often feel compelled to talk about the elephant in the room that everyone else sees but ignores. That's why this issue of authenticity is so important to me. I was born with a very sensitive B.S. button, and anytime a church or ministry presents an advertisement, website, TV program or other presentation that smacks of insincerity, my button lights up.

On my blog at philcooke.com, I've done a number of informal surveys over the years to gauge the reaction of the culture to religious media. In most cases, the issue of authenticity is at the top of the list. Historically, audiences have trouble relating to Christians in media because, although they seem *earnest*, they don't really seem *sincere*. So we have to understand the critical importance of honesty, transparancy, reality and authenticity when we create a brand.

Ultimately, a significant part of being different is being honest about who you are and how you are perceived.

Finding your honest voice in the middle of the media madness is absolutely critical. You don't want to try to duplicate what some other successful ministry leader has done. You need to be absolutely honest about what distinguishes you from the pack. I believe that God made everyone unique, and that's why finding your distinctive combination of gifts and talents is the key to creating your irreplaceable voice.

Gimmicks May Get Attention, but Original Ideas Change the World

This might be a good place to mention the difference between "gimmicks" and "original ideas" when it comes to a brand. This may sound strange, but one of the biggest reasons I work in media ministry today is that growing up, I thought pastors were *so embarrassing*. Being a PK (pastor's kid) in the South during the 1950s the '60s was tough. During that time, pastors would often do some wacky stuff to attract attention or encourage visitors. I remember a pastor who sat perched on a chair atop a three-story-high pole until Sunday attendance hit a certain number; another one locked himself in the steeple, praying for revival. You may remember pastors who shaved their head if the youth program brought enough visitors.

Many of these stunts were innocent; but more than occasionally, it was hard to distinguish some pastors from vaudeville performers. Witnessing to a friend at school was much more difficult when his big question was, "Why does pastor Jones do such stupid things?"

As a result, from an early age, I was incredibly sensitive to gimmicks—the idea that an outrageous stunt or crazy trick would help reach more people with the gospel. Don't get me wrong—most of those pastors and leaders were incredibly sincere. They genuinely wanted to expand the Kingdom and change people's lives. The problem was, they didn't realize what the best and most creative communicators know: *Gimmicks may get attention, but truly original ideas change the world.*

Today, I'm starting to see another wave of gimmicks from a new generation of pastors. Some involve outrageous billboards; others do sex-related stunts; while a few stage mock events in their community—all to get attention and capture that elusive "buzz." The truth is, I love creativity, and I'm wide open to whatever idea you want to float. At the same time, it's important to understand the difference between a *gimmick* and an *original, enduring idea.*

Gimmicks are about short-term gain, not long-term relationships. They get attention, but do they really change people's thinking? Some pastors seem almost addicted to the attention that gimmicks bring. As a result, they look for the most outrageous sermon themes or advertising ideas. But in the age of Lady Gaga, trying to shock an audience with a racy church billboard doesn't really pack much of a punch anymore.

Gimmicks can be dangerous. I'm not talking about falling off that three-story perch. I'm talking about the fact that what's funny to you might be offensive or hurtful to others. In 2010, Spirit Airlines launched the "Check the oil on our beaches" ad campaign. Trying to humorously promote beach destinations not touched by the BP oil spill, they featured photos of bikini-clad women slathered in suntan oil. But they were remarkably tone-deaf to the hundreds of thousands whose jobs were lost and whose lives were devastated by the tragic spill. The public was not amused, and the campaign was quickly pulled.

Gimmicks often backfire. Instead of generating positive press, they often create criticism. Trying to be edgy and cool, McDonald's released the "I'd Hit It" campaign, thinking the phrase meant "choosing it." But the street phrase actually means something much more sexually provocative. Ronald McDonald must have been so proud.

Gimmicks can cheapen your perception and reputation. Ultimately, do you want to be known as a pastor, teacher or leader who taught timeless principles that impacted your community, or as "the guy who preached a sermon in his boxer shorts"?

Pastor Matthew Barnett didn't need a gimmick to build a church that's transforming inner-city Los Angeles. Pastor Mark Jeske didn't need a gimmick to inspire St. Marcus Lutheran Church to create an incredibly successful Christian school in inner-city Milwaukee. Pastor Jack Graham at Prestonwood Church in Plano, Texas, has inspired and launched more entrepreneurial ministries and businesses than perhaps any church in America—and you won't find a trace of a gimmick there.

The list goes on and on . . .

I've spent my career helping churches, ministries and nonprofits be more creative in the way they engage today's cluttered and distracted culture—especially when it comes to media. So I'm certainly not against innovative methods to share your story. So, develop your creative team. Explore unusual ideas. Break some artistic boundaries.

But don't do it at the expense of a gimmick that could undermine your impact.

Take Your **Thinking Deeper**

1. What do people think of when they think of you, your work, your organization or your product?

2. How can the insights I highlight from the book *A Brand Called You* impact your own story?

3. How can you or your organization gain more visibility in your marketplace?

4. Are your message and your organization (and your life) transparent? Do you have anything to hide that an online search might reveal?

5. In what ways do you stand out from the other voices, products or organizations in your space?

Take special time to answer the critical branding questions—preferably with a spouse, close friend or key members of your leadership team. Refer back to the explanations in the text to make sure you understand each question fully:

1. What's the point?
2. Who are you?
3. What are your gifts and talents?
4. What makes you different?

> Don't bring a knife to a gunfight.
> **Anonymous**

> That's a lesson for anybody selling anything—a hamburger, a candidate, or eternal life. It's the connection that counts.
> **Douglas B. Sosnick**
> **Matthew J. Dowd and Ron Fournier**
> *Applebee's America*[1]

The Right Branding Tools

Nearly every week, churches and ministries send copies of their media programs to our office to ask us for advice. *How can we produce our program more effectively? Can you design a new logo for us? Can you help us with our lighting? What about our editing?* Usually the questions come from pastors or ministry leaders frustrated about the poor quality of their television outreach.

The truth is, a significant number of churches and ministries produce very poor programming without realizing that the lack of quality is a huge obstacle to viewers. In the early days of television, people were fascinated that they could see a program at all. Broadcast "snow," poor audio or bad lighting didn't bother them, because the new medium was such a marvel.

But in an HD (high definition) world, with hundreds of channels, the competition is so great with most cable or satellite television systems that the slightest problem with quality causes viewers to find another program. That's why choosing the right medium for your message, and using the right tools, is a key part of the branding puzzle. In fact, many potential breakthrough talents in ministry today are terribly obscured because they preach their message through the wrong medium or with faulty tools.

Quality Versus Response

One of the most-asked questions I receive is, "Once I create a strong brand, will producing programs, especially commercial spots and product offers with higher production quality, get a higher response?"

There's no real way to know. In my experience the results have been around 50/50. Sometimes the higher quality cuts through the television clutter and connects with the audience, causing them to respond. But at other times, a poorly produced version gets the same and sometimes better response.

From time to time, I've seen ministries create poorly produced programs that still get a terrific response. Later, when they have the money and they update the program to a higher level of professionalism and quality, the response actually drops.

After producing programming for more than three decades, I've learned that in spite of marketing tools, research and sophisticated production techniques, sometimes there is no discernible reason that people connect with a certain type of program or product.

On the other hand, I've also discovered that if you want to keep an audience for the long haul, quality is the only way to go.

*A higher-quality production might
not generate a better response at the moment,
but it will impact the overall perception
of your ministry.*

The key reason to produce at the highest and most contemporary level possible is that you're creating a long-term perception in the eyes of your audience. Certainly, the content of a single product or commercial may resonate with the audience, causing them to respond regardless of the production quality. But there's no question that over the long haul, quality always wins out. Plus, a new generation is watching that is more media savvy than ever and tuned in to quality. If you want to make an impression with them, a badly written, produced or directed program simply won't cut it.

It's a matter of the brand story you want to leave in the mind of your audience, church members or supporters. Keep in mind our original question in the introduction:

What do people think of when they think of you?

So, what do great communicators know about their tools that others don't?

1. The Medium Is the Message

The first time I encountered the subject of "mass communication studies" was as a college freshman in the fall of 1972. At that time, the writings and lectures of Canadian academic and writer Marshall McLuhan were all the rage on college campuses, and our professor was one of his most ardent disciples. By all accounts, McLuhan was brilliant. He was fluent in seven languages, held a Ph.D. from Cambridge in English Literature, and received at least 10 honorary doctorates in his lifetime.

McLuhan's *The Gutenberg Galaxy: The Making of Typographic Man* appeared in 1962, followed by *Understanding Media: The Extensions of Man* in 1964, *The Medium Is the Message* in 1967, and *War and Peace in the Global Village* in 1968. He generally wrote his books as collages of short statements or interviews, and he made numerous media appearances, including a spot in Woody Allen's 1977 comedy *Annie Hall*.

But it was his seminal book *Understanding Media: The Extensions of Man* that was regarded as the holy grail of culture studies. He coined the terms "Global Village" and "Age of Information" long before the Internet, and his work has inspired some of the greatest media pioneers of our time.

I had no idea during those years that McLuhan was actually a devout Catholic, and it was his faith that drove much of his work on the media frontier. Back in the early seventies, he believed that centralized Christianity was losing its power, and he predicted the loose-networked movement of independent churches—even megachurches—long before most people considered the possibility.

The most powerful of McLuhan's pronouncements was the statement that *the medium is the message*. In other words, the medium we choose to deliver a message has a significant impact on the message itself. In the church, we often say that the method may change, but the message doesn't. I've heard that phrase over and over again as a clarion call to continually embrace technology and new media in an effort to keep the gospel message alive in the culture.

It sounds good, but if McLuhan is right, it's not true at all. Perhaps the most significant expression of this thinking is his statement, "The content or message of any particular medium has about as much importance as the stenciling on the casing of an atomic bomb." He felt that the medium used to deliver the message is actually far more important than the message itself.

That's pretty tough, but it's worth serious consideration.

> Each time technology develops a
> new medium, it's not simply an extension
> of the last; it's far more—it's a completely new
> and different entity.

Program writers, directors and producers found this out during the early days between the transition from radio to television. When television was first invented, most dramatic scripts were simply radio dramas with pictures. In other words, there wasn't much visual action; directors just shot actors standing around talking to each other. It was flat and lifeless, and the audience wasn't impressed.

That's when someone finally recognized that television was something altogether new. That realization paved the way for what we now call "The Golden Years of Television." That was the period roughly from 1949 to 1960 that is still considered one of the greatest eras of television programming.

In his book *Amusing Ourselves to Death*, media critic Neil Postman discusses the impact that form has over content:

> To take a simple example of what this means, consider the primitive technology of smoke signals. While I do not know exactly what content was once carried in the smoke signals of American Indians, I can safely guess that it did not include philosophical argument. Puffs of smoke are insufficiently complex to express ideas on the nature of existence, and even if they were not, a Cherokee philosopher would run short of either wood or blankets long before he reached his second axiom. You cannot use smoke to do philosophy. Its form excludes the content.[2]

Would Jesus Have Left the Dead Sea Videotapes?

In 1977, British journalist Malcolm Muggeridge echoed McLuhan and Postman when he wrote *Christ and the Media*. His purpose was to examine whether or not Jesus, had He been born in the present day, would have left the Dead Sea Videotapes rather than the Dead Sea Scrolls. Muggeridge was very careful to point out that directing, shooting, lighting and editing techniques can be so manipulated that television is inherently a lie.

He speaks from experience, recounting a remarkable story:

> The most horrifying example I know of the camera's power and authority, which will surely be in the history books as an example of the degradation our servitude to it can

involve, occurred in Nigeria at the time of the Biafran War. A prisoner was to be executed by a firing squad, and the cameras turned up in force to photograph and film the scene. Just as the command to fire was about to the given, one of the cameramen shouted "Cut!"; his battery had gone dead and needed to be replaced. Until this was done, the execution stood suspended. Then, with his battery working again, he shouted "Action!," and bang, bang, the prisoner fell to the ground, his death duly recorded, to be shown in millions of sitting rooms throughout the so-called civilized world. Some future historian may speculate as to where lay the greatest barbarism, on the part of the viewers, the executioners, or the camera. I think myself that he would plump for the cameras.[3]

Muggeridge admits that we shouldn't throw out technology altogether, but he does give a caution that's worth considering:

It's very nearly impossible to tell the truth in television, but you can try very hard. As far as the word is concerned, spoken or written, it has been used, and continues to be used, for purposes of deception, and for evil purposes like pornography. This is absolutely true. But, you see, a word comes from a man. Putting it in its simplest terms, if I write a novel, signed by my name, I am saying these are my thoughts, these are my views, these are my impressions, and the response of the reader is according. If you set up a camera and take a film, that is not considered to be any-body's views; that is reality, and, of course, it is much more fantasy than the words. Supposing there had been a film made of the life of our Lord. Do you think that that would have stirred men as the Gospels have?[4]

I respect Muggeridge's views because of his credentials as a journalist and Christian. He presents us a balance but also gives us reasons for great caution as well. As a journalist of his era, he was a print man, no question, and found the transition to film and video challenging at best.

He once wrote about a story by Soviet labor camp survivor Alexander Solzhenitsyn, about a desperate man in the bunk above his who "used to climb up into it in the evening, and take old, much-folded pieces of paper out of his pocket, and read them with evident satisfaction. It turned out that they had passages from the Gospels scribbled on them, which were his solace and joy in that terrible place. He would not, I feel sure, have been similarly comforted and edified by re-runs of old footage of religious TV programs."[5]

The Media Disconnect

From time to time, various network news programs are interested in my opinion about issues of media, faith and culture. Sometimes it revolves around a new movie, a political issue, or a religious controversy. We normally think of these shows on cable networks like Fox News, CNN, or MSNBC as legitimate news programs, sparking debate and discussion on contemporary issues; but I soon discovered the exasperating limitations.

Because of my busy travel schedule, I'm usually asked to come to a local TV station or news affiliate in whatever city I'm in so that they can connect to me live via satellite for the interview. After arriving, I'm ushered into a small black room with a single TV camera pointed at my chair. No TV monitors are in the room, so I can't actually see the program host or the other guests against whom I might be debating.

In addition, I rarely even know what points will be discussed or the experts I might be up against. The host or hostess completely controls the interview, and without being able to see anyone, I'm totally dependent on the earpiece that connects me to the program's audio track.

The most difficult part to navigate in these interviews is that I have no idea how many times I'll be able to respond to an issue, or if my current comment will be my last. So the actual development of a line of thought is impossible, and the best I can hope for is a fragment or soundbite that makes sense. Worse, I occasionally have to confront a belligerent guest, so anything I say has to be timed between his or her tirades.

During her days on CNN, I was featured on Paula Zahn's program multiple times, and she's a brilliant and gracious journalist. When I'm on the air, we're like friends, but I've never actually met her or spoken one word to her outside my actual time live on the broadcast.

Such is the nature of the medium and the resulting impact on political and cultural discourse.

Do we toss out technology? No. But the writings of McLuhan, Postman and Muggeridge teach us that we can't be too careful in how we present an eternal message on a temporal medium. The medium does indeed impact the message.

2. Choose the Right Medium

When William Tyndale translated the Bible into English in the sixteenth century, it changed the course of history. And yet, it would have made far less impact if he hadn't understood the power of the right medium.

Due to the limitations of printing, most books were very large and heavy. Think of the old 20-pound family Bible you might have grown up with and you'll get the idea. They were also bound in leather, which made owning books too expensive for most people. As a result, only scholars and the very rich read books on a regular basis. In fact, books were so expensive and rare that many were actually chained to pulpits at church or desks in libraries.

Tyndale knew that for his translation to have impact, it would have to be read by thousands of people, so he published his English New Testament in a smaller-sized version that anyone could carry around in his pocket. It was the first time a Bible had been printed in such small dimensions, and it became a sensation. During Tyndale's lifetime, it was illegal to own a Bible in the English language, so the convenience of its size made it easy to hide. It wasn't long before thousands of these translations were being published and read secretly throughout the British Isles.

Because Tyndale understood the power of the right medium, his impact cannot be measured.

What is it about your message that works particularly well on television? Would it be better as a radio program, podcast or a video clip on the church website? Television certainly gets a lot of attention, but increasingly, it's not the only game in town.

Today the number of video downloads from sites like YouTube compete with the audience numbers of prime-time television networks. A line has clearly been crossed, and there's a significant audience out there that most churches, ministries and nonprofits know little or nothing about.

Even if you choose television as your medium, a weekly 30-minute program may not be the answer. I had one client in the Midwest who was a pastor with a heart to reach men. Realizing that another 30-minute weekly program wouldn't help separate him from the ministry pack, he started producing 30-*second* spots and used them to sponsor the sports report on the local evening TV news. As a result, he's reaching more men during those 30-second breaks than all the full-length Christian programs in his market combined. He writes the spots around male-oriented subjects and speaks into the lives of thousands of men every night during the sports news report.

It's a perfect example of thinking differently and being innovative in a competitive market.

How Does It Look on Your Mobile Device?
Whatever video content you choose, remember this: *platforms matter*. Watching a TV program on my 60-inch HDTV screen is dramatically different than watching it on my iPhone screen. Years ago, directors understood the difference between shooting movies for the theater screen and shooting them for television. They knew

that wide, panoramic shots looked fantastic on a giant movie screen; but once that movie played on a much smaller TV set, all that detail was lost. So directors began using more close-ups and tighter shots if they were shooting a TV movie or episodic series.

In the same way, directing video content for multiple platforms in today's digital world has become an art form. A video played on your huge image magnification screens at church will look one way; but a video played on a handheld mobile device is something else entirely.

Know the difference. It could make a dramatic impact on how your presentation is received by the viewer.

Cultural Sensitivity

The medium used can also be heavily influenced by the cultural setting. Think of how TV is viewed in the United States versus a country like China, where broadcasting is extremely regulated and censored. In the Middle East, satellite dishes litter rooftops, even in countries where watching the wrong networks can result in imprisonment. Under those constraints, media use takes on a completely different character.

While teaching in Russia a few years ago, I was dismayed to find so many American TV ministries broadcasting the same programs throughout Eastern Europe as they broadcast in Cleveland or Kansas City. Audiences in China, Iraq or the Sudan don't watch programs through the same lens as we do, not to mention illustrations, commercials and segments that viewers outside the United States wouldn't comprehend.

When MTV exploded globally a number of years ago, one of the first strategies they implemented was to open local bureaus in major countries around the world. They knew that the key to success was cultural sensitivity; so they focused MTV-India on local musicians and artists and did the same in various geographic regions throughout the world. Today, MTV's programming is different for each country in which it is viewed; as a result, their global fan base is staggering.

One of the few Christian TV networks to follow that example is the SAT-7 Network in the Middle East. Because they are broadcasting via satellite primarily to Arab audiences in the Middle East and North Africa, they rely primarily on local programming that resonates with the interests and needs of their audience.

Earlier in the book, I told the story of my perception problem with a skeptical customs agent in Manaus, Brazil. When he finally let us pick up our gear, we headed deep into the Amazon rain forest. After chartering a light plane to go deeper into the jungle and negotiating a river freighter to take us two more days upriver, we finally moved our equipment to canoes for the last day's journey near the headwaters of the legendary river. It would be no stretch to say we were about as far from civilization as you could imagine.

Our task was to film a remote Brazilian tribe; but when we arrived in the village, it was deserted. There were six crude thatched huts in the clearing, and we walked carefully from hut to hut, looking for any sign of life. When we finally came to the last shelter, to our shock and surprise, we discovered that all the villagers were crammed into the small hut, crowded around a beat-up black-and-white TV set powered by a dying car battery.

They were watching a static-filled broadcast, from who knows where, of the 1978–1991 American television series *Dallas*. I stood there in stunned amazement, wondering what these isolated tribesmen thought of J. R. and Sue Ellen, and how that knowledge would potentially screw up their perceptions and culture for years to come.

The medium impacts the message, and the medium is viewed differently in diverse locations and cultures. Choosing the right medium for the message and the right medium for the audience is critical. For whatever situation, we need to be extremely careful in the media platform we select.

3. Get the Right Advice

One of the great frustrations of my career has been seeing great churches and religious organizations crippled because of the wrong advice. Advancing technology has caused the price of audio and video equipment to tumble dramatically during the last 30 years, but don't be fooled—creating a major national media outreach is still an expensive proposition.

Today, outsourcing is all the rage in corporate America. The theory behind the practice is worth thinking about: If there is some aspect of your business that you don't do well, then outsource it to someone who does. For instance, a corporation that builds computers might not be so strong at strategic planning; or a company that manufactures sports equipment probably doesn't understand marketing and public relations. So they find consultants with experience and success in those areas to give them advice, training and expertise.

Could churches, ministries and other Christian organizations benefit from the concept?

Absolutely.

Although our mandate for reaching the world couldn't be simpler, the various ways available to accomplish that mandate couldn't be more complex. Today, churches and ministries routinely use new technology, the media, branding, marketing strategies, leadership training and other tools to make their outreaches, educational programs and ministries more successful.

That's why thousands of churches and parachurch ministries around the world use consultants (experts in particular fields) to help them understand and implement their outreaches more effectively. Consultants are available in areas such as Christian education, computer technology, TV and radio production, post-production, media, strategic planning, broadcast engineering, leadership, branding, marketing and advertising, and more; and they can make a real difference in raising the level of competence for your staff members, employees and leaders.

In the secular world, client-consultant relationships work for years, and even decades. In television production, for instance, it might take years to build or reshape your television outreach, especially at a national level. Training a crew, buying the right equipment, selecting the best TV stations and networks, building a fund-raising program, developing a long-term media strategy, branding your program, advertising and promotion, graphic design, exploring international media opportunities, and more, take time. Sometimes a consultant can come in and fix something right away, but that's the exception rather than the rule. Look for a consultant who can provide long-term advice and planning to help you achieve your goals; and make sure he has the staff, resources and tools for staying with you for the long haul to take your church or ministry to the far reaches of success and effectiveness.

Ask the Right Questions

Here are some important questions to answer about the tools you are using:

- What *traditional* media are you currently using (film, TV, print, radio)?
- What *digital* media tools are you currently using (website, blogs, video, social media, podcasting, mobile apps, streaming media, online communities)?
- Based on the evidence, what medium delivers your message most effectively?
- What are your media frustrations?
- What are your media opportunities?
- What audience are you trying to reach?
- What media platforms is your unique audience using the most?
- Why do you want to use the media? (What do you hope can be accomplished?)

The Branded Building

One area that a handful of pastors and ministry leaders have maximized is the concept of using architecture to impact the brand.

Pastor Greg Laurie's Harvest Church in Riverside, California, has created a public meeting place that looks like a cross between Barnes & Noble, Starbucks and the city square. You can have lunch, buy a book or CD, drink gourmet coffee, or sit in the California sun and relax. It has become so popular that people who would never darken the door of the church on Sunday gladly drop in during the week for lunch. The contemporary design welcomes visitors, and the practicality makes them feel at home.

Years ago, mega-churches took a lot of flak for building a coffee bar in the lobby or expanding restaurants and shops; but the truth is, these churches understood the importance of building community as part of the brand. It makes a particular impact among young people, who are trying to initiate connections of their own and are looking for places to meet.

Douglas B. Sosnick, Matthew J. Dowd and Ron Fournier relate their conversation with Starbucks founder Howard Schultz in their book *Applebee's America*, as he described how that company discovered the power of community:

> The desire for atmosphere and camaraderie was most intense among people in their twenties who had grown up with no safe place to hang out other than shopping malls, Schultz told us in 2006. As young adults, some found bars too noisy and threatening for companionship. So they hung out in cars and coffee bars. Other trends of the 1990s helped Starbucks, including the growing number of people who worked from home and used coffee shops as a second office. It helped that the Internet was becoming a part of the culture at the same time that Schultz was making Starbucks part of it too. Wireless access to the Internet helped make coffee shops a Third Place. "We have evolved and taken advantage of changes in the way people work and how they live in their homes, and, most of all, the fact that people are very hungry for human contact," Schultz told us. "I think it's a new phenomenon. I think if you kind of

get underneath the rise in technology and the way people use personal electronic devices, it has become a secular way in which people act, and that has led to people's desires to have some degree of human contact during the day, and Starbucks has definitely benefited from that."[6]

Notice how many areas Schultz reacted and connected to, because he was always aware of the changes in the culture. He first recognized the need for *place*. So he built a company that didn't just sell a product but also created a safe and comfortable place where people found community. He used architecture as the starting point of building the brand.

Second, he saw the *rise in home-based workers*, so he made the shops a functional place to work. Third, as he watched *the rise in the Internet's popularity*, he made wireless access a priority. Finally, he recognized the need in people's lives for a "Third Place." That's the place you want to be after home and work, and it's the Holy Grail of many retailers. As a boy growing up in the South, my Third Place was church. We had activities of all kinds throughout the week, because it was a real focal point for the community. The church lost that position beginning in the sixties; but now, pastors are seeing the possibilities of reclaiming that spot in people's lives.

Because Howard Schultz was aware of these changes happening in the culture, he responded with the Starbucks brand and accommodated each of these needs, making the chain of coffee shops the most popular in the world. We don't have to be technology slaves, but we do need to see the changes happening in the culture and recognize how we can respond with our brand.

Branding extends even into the details of the building. Starbucks selected round tables because studies indicated that a single person sitting at a square table makes them look and feel more alone. They also discovered that round tables made the coffee shop flow more from a design point of view. Because a sense of community is important for Starbucks, anything that made people feel alone and separated had to be eliminated or at least toned down to a minimum.

The right tools are the gateway to expressing your brand identity to the world. Whether you use church bulletins, highway billboards, websites, radio, television, podcasting, social media, architecture or something else, using the wrong tools or using them ineffectively will blur your story and contaminate your identity. Create a clear vision for your audience and express that vision from the highest quality launching pad possible.

A great brand will always be hurt by poor communication; and without the right tools, you'll never reach your largest potential audience.

The Power of "Buzz"

In the religious community, we often forget the single greatest result of powerful branding: word of mouth advertising, or "buzz." It could be argued that Joel Osteen sold millions of copies of his first book *Your Best Life Now* because of the remarkable success of his weekly television program. TV ratings services report that he's the most watched inspirational program on television, with millions of viewers each week. In addition, Joel regularly preaches around the country in massive arenas and sports stadiums that hold tens of thousands of people in standing-room-only crowds. The meetings have been so successful that the largest arenas have required that Joel's ministry sell tickets in order to control the throngs willing to stand in line for hours just to get a seat. As a result of that national promotion, his books sell in significant numbers.

Joel's momentum is remarkable.

Years ago, I talked with Joel about his podcast on iTunes. In just a matter of months from the date it was first released, it rose to number nine nationally on the iTunes site. That's the power of momentum in action. We discussed that he doesn't charge customers for the podcast, but it has enormous value because of ubiquity—the fact of being everywhere. In the world of branding, being everywhere is gold. His TV program, his books, his live events, his website and social media strategy—and now his podcast—give him a platform in multiple arenas for his audience to connect with. That combined momentum of multiple locations extends the power of his brand.

Joyce Meyer is no different. Her daily television program is a huge success and, like Joel, she takes her ministry on the road and fills auditoriums and arenas across the country each month. Her best-seller books, like *Battlefield of the Mind* and *Approval Addiction*, are driven in large part by her success on television.

Spreading your message across multiple media platforms is an important key to creating and maintaining the all-illusive "buzz."

If You Don't Have Mass Media on Your Side

What about Rick Warren's book *The Purpose Driven Life*? Rick doesn't have a television program, and he doesn't do major arena events on a regular basis. What drove his book to sell more than 30 million copies?

Many would point to his pastors' network and his regular email correspondence with thousands of church leaders. But he has built that network without national radio, TV or even print promotion. His success is an example of the power of *word of mouth* advertising. People telling other people about your product, church or organization is a powerful tool.

We live in an age of *influencers*, with some researchers saying that at least 1 out of every 10 people is someone the other 9 ask for advice on any number of issues—from restaurants, movies, cars, shopping, churches, and more.

After all, we're drowning in information, and people are looking for answers they can trust. As of this writing, in America there are:

- More than 13,000 radio stations
- More than 1,300 TV stations
- More than 18,000 magazines
- More than 390 cable networks

- Hundreds more pay-per-view channels
- Billions of websites and online blogs

In Los Angeles alone, combining broadcast stations, cable and pay-per-view, I have nearly 500 channels coming into my home. Plus, I still have piles of DVDs to get to as well as movies waiting on my TiVo.

If my wife, Kathleen, has an addiction, it's magazine subscriptions. She's a sucker for every school kid who drops by selling subscriptions (please don't let the word out); and as a result, we have numerous piles of magazines lined up throughout the house. When I travel, I take as many magazines as I can cram into a large bag just to catch up.

My weakness is books. I've inherited that from my father, so maybe I have an excuse. But my library is getting into the thousands with no sign of letting up, and I have stacks of unread books just waiting for me to attack.

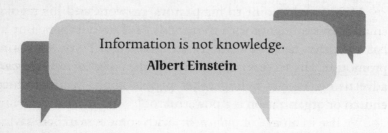

Information is not knowledge.
Albert Einstein

We're surrounded by more and more information, and like lost tourists in unknown territory, we desperately need a guide. We always thought the digital revolution would help us leave our shackles of ignorance behind; but now more than ever we've become slaves to technology and the flood of data it has created. Who can possibly make an intelligent choice when so much is thrown at us each day?

In a world of media clutter, who can you trust?

Your friends.

That's why friends sharing with each other the news about your church, ministry or nonprofit is so important.

Research indicates that the single most trusted source for guidance on any number of important issues is another person. Personal relationships help people connect to church, medical services, entertainment, products and a multitude of other important issues.

Taking your message directly to the people is a key part of successful branding. When Toyota launched their Scion automobile to the Gen Y crowd, instead of massive national advertising, they selectively put a number of the cars on major college campuses across the country. No advertising, no salespeople, no brochures, nothing.

Seeing the unique-looking cars sitting in parking lots without fanfare or promotion intrigued these kids who had grown up distrustful of regular advertising. So instead of the traditional method of flooding the market with advertising and promotion, Toyota kept the cool factor alive by leaking information out gradually and allowing student influencers to talk it up.

Throughout Malcolm Gladwell's book *The Tipping Point: How Little Things Can Make a Big Difference*, he cites numerous examples of strategic marketing where companies let the influencers guide the conversation with friends and co-workers. Some give out free samples of products to people they know will talk it up. Others stage parties or other events and invite people who will use their influence to promote the product or service. Others focus on returning customers, who feel like part of an insider club and eagerly share this new product with friends and co-workers.

The buzz approach helps in two ways: First, it's perfect if you have a limited budget (and what church, ministry or nonprofit doesn't?). Second, it gives the product credibility, since it's being recommended by a trusted friend.

I'm convinced that's why personal testimonies work so well in the media. In our experience with producing infomercials and direct-response advertising, the phones light up after a personal testimony about the product or organization. We've discovered that a program host or hostess can talk about a product until they're blue in the face, but when the viewer actually sees John Q. Public talking about how the product has changed his life, he apparently thinks, *If it works for him, maybe it will work for me.*

Hearing from another person is critical. So in your branding efforts, include testimonies so that your audience can hear from real people how the product or organization has impacted them.

Ultimately, it's about trust. People are growing ever more skeptical about what they are hearing on television or from politicians. However, when they hear it from a friend, something rings true.

This is especially true for a younger generation that grew up with advertising. Today's teenagers have been pitched everything and are naturally far more skeptical than any other generation in history. They've seen the cons, heard the trash and read the spam. What they see in the media makes them wary, so they naturally turn to friends for the real deal on everything from the latest movie to the new cell phones or the hot new restaurant in town.

One great *digital* tool for promoting buzz is social media. For years we've been telling our clients to encourage all their supporters to talk up their work through Twitter, Facebook, blogs and other social media channels. Even with small organizations, it can spark significant online conversations, flooding the Web with positive stories about the ministry.

And in a digital age, what better way to invite people to church? Pastors, when was the last time you asked your congregation to share their worship experiences online? And don't forget review sites like Yelp.com. Social media is about listening to trusted friends, and they talk about everything else, so why not church? Remember: The more online activity created about an organization, the more that organization moves to the top of search engine results, and the more people find you.

In the middle of your excitement about national advertising and promotions, never forget the simple things, like taking your message directly to the people who can help you the most.

Take Your **Thinking Deeper**

1. Think about how different media impact your message. What are the challenges in presenting your message at a live event versus radio, TV, the Internet or social media? How do different platforms have an impact on the message itself?

2. What is the optimum media for sharing your particular message? Budget certainly matters, but never let that be your only criterion. If you could have any opportunity, would you launch a social media campaign? Write a blog? Produce a short film? Create a weekly TV program? Write a book? Produce a feature film or documentary? What's the absolute best way to get the word out about your message, product or organization?

3. Is your website optimized for a mobile device? Is it easy to navigate, or is it frustrating for users?

4. This is your message and your life—take it seriously. Who are you getting your communications and media advice from? Is it an experienced professional with a proven track record, or a well-intentioned but less than knowledgeable friend or co-worker?

5. Who is the right media strategist, producer or consultant that can get you from where you are to where you want to be?

6. How about your building? What does its design say about your message? How does it engage a visitor?

Why Social Media Matters

> The end goal of all our social media efforts is that people connect with God and find real face-to-face community in a local church. Twitter has created some significant ministry moments. Via Twitter we have ministered to women in other countries fighting eating disorders, prayed with people who just lost a loved one, shared the gospel and helped people outside of LA find a local church home.
>
> **Kristen Tarsiuk**
> Communications Director, Oasis Church in Los Angeles

> To get your message out, you have to put it EVERYWHERE. After doing a huge direct-mail campaign and mentioning an event everywhere we thought possible, we still had someone say, "I'm so glad you posted this on Facebook or I never would have known about it!"
>
> **Katy Klinnert**
> Creative Media Strategist,
> Time of Grace Ministry in Milwaukee

More People Than You Can Imagine Are Waiting to Share Your Story

Every brand should be a gospel. It's "good news" to someone, whether that "someone" is the company shareholders, donors, audience, congregation, or the people who "buy" a product. Essentially, a brand survives based on the goodness it offers. But a brand *grows* based on how well that goodness interacts with people's lives. Hundreds and thousands of *good* products, humanitarian efforts, movies, books, or Sunday worship experiences exist in the world. Yet they don't grow beyond their current size because they don't participate in the lives outside their immediate influence. This doesn't make them a failure. It just keeps them and their stories limited and confined.

What these *good-yet-confined* brands don't capitalize on is that people, everyday people, want to participate in good things. However, in order for people to do that, we must first take our brand to them—in other words—*connect*. A *good* brand—a good story—must participate in the stories of others in order to invite them to write new chapters in our brand's gospel. Social media is a way to do just that.

> ## Social media is a digital connection to effectively invite others to participate in our stories by first participating in theirs.

A generation ago, the only way to share your story was in print (books, magazines, brochures), through traditional mass media (radio, TV, movies), or in live events (sermons, crusades, rallies). All of those options were either expensive or took a significant organization to make happen. Today, we live in a different world—the world of social media. It's a world where *influence* has been turned upside down.

In this chapter, we're going to discuss what makes social media so effective. Then we'll look at how your brand can use social media to participate in the lives of others and invite them to invest in your story.

Before we get to that, let me offer some quick insight into what everyone is talking about when they use the words "social media." When Green Bay Packer football coach Vince Lombardi started each season, he gathered his team around him in the locker room. In that group were the greatest players in the game, including legends such as Bart Starr and Paul Hornung. But in spite of their experience, Lombardi started the meeting by holding up a football and saying, "Gentlemen, this is a football."

He understood the power of starting with the fundamentals.

If you are an experienced social media user, forgive me for starting with the basics. For newcomers, it never hurts to start at the beginning.

The Development of Social Media

Social media, as a whole, is not Facebook. It's not Twitter. It's not Pinterest. It's not blogs or social bookmarks or geo-tracking, or any of the terms you may have heard in contemporary discussions about the Internet. Just as a brick is *part* of a house, Facebook, Twitter, blogging and the like are part of the greater domain of social media. All together, they form a valuable approach to a world connected through the Internet.

---

blog (bläg): A "blog" (a contraction of the terms "web" and "log") is a type of website usually maintained by an individual who writes regular entries or commentaries, descriptions of events or other material such as graphics or videos. A handful of websites exist where, for free, anyone can set up a personal blog and reprogram the template in order to create their own look. Popular examples of sites like this are Wordpress.com, Blogger.com, and Tumblr.com. So many companies and individuals actually use WordPress templates for their company site that it may be more appropriate to refer to these forms of social media as "content management."

When the Internet began to take shape in the 1960s, it was first imagined as a private, protected system to be used mostly in government, academic or military communication. As time went on, this technology became more public, breaking forward in 1992, when the first commercial email system and full Internet services were offered to everyday consumers.[1] By 2010, it was estimated that nearly 80 percent of the U.S. population used the

Internet.[2] Between 1992 and 2010, the Internet skyrocketed because people capitalized on its best quality—the ability to connect with other people. As Katy Klinnert, Creative Media Strategist at Time of Grace Ministries in Milwaukee, has said, "On an average Sunday, you might get a churchgoer's attention for an hour or two. But since Nielsen [the Nielsen ratings] tells us that U.S. Internet users spend more time on Facebook than any other website, how much of their captive time during the week are you missing out on if you're only reaching out on Sunday mornings?"

> Right now, a Maasai warrior on a mobile phone has better mobile communications than [the president of the United States] did 25 years ago; and, if they're on Google, they have access to more information than the president did just 15 years ago. They are effectively living in a world of communications and information abundance.
>
> **Peter Diamandis and Steven Kotler**
> *Abundance: The Future Is Better Than You Think*

Since day one, social media has had a very strong allure. I remember taking an early laptop on the road and packing a small toolkit that allowed me to open up my hotel room's phone jack and hook up my crude modem. It was incredibly slow and, truthfully, I only knew a small handful of people I could connect to anyway, but it was exhilarating.

The future was here.

Today, social media has exploded in the form of a multitude of Internet-based platforms that utilize this connection by allowing people to share their stories in a social manner that was once possible only in person. Through the Internet, people can share their opinions on any topic (from politics to a celebrity's hairstyle); photos of their family at the beach; what newspaper article they read that morning or what musical artist they are currently listening to; or (horrors!) a cat video. There are limitless possibilities. While people can share this social information about themselves, other people can interact by posting their own comments in response. This creates an online dialogue with the potential to interact with hundreds of people at once; hence, the format is called *social* media.

If you are of a certain age, you will recall, with some pain, the hours you used to sit through a friend's slide show of his or her summer vacation. BF (Before Facebook), if I wanted to show you my daughter's wedding album, you had to come over to my house and look through the entire book. Now I can simply add a selection of the photos (or all of them) to my online photo collection on Flickr or another photo site, tell people I've added the photos online via a post on Twitter or Facebook, and then comment on my blog about my experience as a father of the bride. At the same time, my wife has probably posted photos of our daughter's wedding dress on Pinterest for her friends to see.

Facebook (fās/buk): A social network site where users can join networks of other users organized by city, workplace, school and region to connect and interact. A user has a personal profile, which includes photos, information ranging from past jobs to favorite television shows, and a "wall" on the profile where friends can post comments, pictures, and the like. Each user has a current "status" they can update to say anything they want. They'll write about what they're thinking, who they're with, where they are or post a URL link to another website they've been looking at. Users build their networks by adding other users as "friends" and by clicking a "like" icon for companies and other organizations that have a Facebook "fan" page. Facebook was created by Mark Zuckerberg while he was a student at Harvard. He's the poster child for social media and a name to remember from this era.

If I'm strategic about where, how and when I post about the wedding, I could have (1) my blog featured on a dozen bridal websites, (2) my wedding photographers gathering more business from people who have seen my daughter's album, (3) an outreach to soon-to-be fathers of the bride who comment on my blog, and (4) hundreds of more "friends" and "followers" to my personal or corporate Facebook and Twitter accounts. That's why the phrase "going viral" has become such an apt description of online activity.

How Worthwhile Is Social Media?

Social media is an effective use of your brand's resources because of *numbers* and *values*. Mass *numbers* of people participate in social media every minute because it strikes a chord in the area of core qualities we *value* in human interaction.

Here's a look at some of the numbers:

- By the end of 2011, Facebook reported 845 million monthly active users, 80 percent of whom are outside the United States and Canada.[3]

- By the start of 2012, Twitter reported 140 million active users, with 400 million tweets per day. Note that this is only 6 years after it was created. Over its lifetime to that point, Twitter had seen 532 million accounts registered. Also, only one-third of the website's traffic comes from the U.S.[4]

- Wordpress.com (a popular form of free blogging and content management) boasts that there are more than 72 million WordPress sites in the world—including my own at philcooke.com. These 355 million people view more than 2.5 billion pages each month on these sites. On average, about 500,000 new blog posts are published each day, with 400,000 new comments written about those posts.[5]

- There are over 46 million blogs on Tumblr.com (a free site for micro-blogging, geared toward shorter blog posts).[6]

- It's also estimated that there are currently 1.2 billion social media users worldwide, and that 1 out of every 5 minutes spent online is on a social networking site. Also, the average American spends 5.7 hours per month on social networking through social media.[7]

It's important to note that while social media sites like Facebook and Twitter report large numbers, that doesn't mean each one of those people uses his or her accounts frequently, if at all. There are four types of users on social networking sites. *Casual* users occasionally check the site but don't participate with new comments or likes. They also rarely update their Facebook status or tweets. In fact, this is a majority of reported users on Facebook. Some users can even be classified as *ghosts*. That is, they have a profile but they don't have a personal photo or any information about themselves or any signs of interaction with anyone.

Twitter (twi/tər): A social networking and micro-blogging service that enables its users to send and read other users' updates known as "tweets." Tweets are text-based posts of up to 140 characters in length that are posted on a user's profile page. Twitter users build their networks by becoming "followers" of other users. As followers, they can interact with each other's posts. Users can include other users in a tweet by using an @ followed by your Twitter name. The tagged person can then see that they have been re-tweeted. Users will also use a # to "hashtag" (or mark) their tweets. For example, if I made a post about one of my previous books, I would end the post with #onebigthing or #jolt. There are millions of hashtags, from #ihateschoolbecause to #celebritybloopers. Most people search for more common hashtags like #leadership, #God, or #success. Later, people could do a search for comments people are making about those subjects, and the hashtag would help them find tweets from among hundreds or thousands of others on the same subject.

The fact that ghosts and casual users comprise such a large number of users would be concerning if the goal of social media was to simply get eyeballs to notice your brand. Casual users seeing your brand may have an effect like a billboard ad, which, of course, is something. But that's not the point, because people can't interact with a billboard like they can with a brand through social media.

What Makes Social Media So Effective

At its core, social media is a *conversation,* and the same etiquette rules apply. The real power of social media is in engaging with people who take interest in interacting with your brand. This *interactive* group comprises at least a quarter of the social network users, which are still very large numbers at the end of the day.

Interactive users will post their own opinions, photos, videos they're watching, and links to websites and news articles they find interesting. They'll post things they find offensive in order to criticize them (such as provocative commercials for politicians, or photos of mean-spirited TV evangelists). This crowd is also interested in dialoguing with companies. They will not only "like" a company but will take the time to post comments to that company and re-post a post the company made.

Interactive social media users are the ones who check their Facebook or post tweets from their laptops at coffee shops or in classrooms and company meetings. They often have mobile devices that have applications that connect to their Facebook, Twitter or other sites when they're not near a computer. With these "apps," they can post pictures and comments about where they are and who else they're with. As an example of geo-locating, interactive users will "check in" when they arrive at a restaurant or store or club or church. (Foursquare.com is a popular social media site dedicated to just this.) Sometimes they're simply announcing their presence and telling their friends and followers where they are. Sometimes they're doing it to tell the company where they are in hopes that the company offers coupons or interacts with them.

If you're trying to create a social media strategy for how to engage such interactive people, that makes you an *intentional* social media user. That category includes brands, companies and individuals who utilize social networking sites to gather an audience in order to reach particular objectives. This doesn't mean that all of them do it well. Many intentional users approach social media like it's the latest fashion trend or cool thing that all the kids are into these days. They get caught up with just the number of users on social media and not the strategy it requires to *engage* people.

As the *Economist* magazine pointed out, with 845 million users around the world, from the perspective of population, Facebook is the third largest country behind China and India. This begs the following questions:

Why are we not sending missionaries to that country?

Why are we not planting churches there?

> In the online age, Christian organizations need to stop thinking of "missions" solely in terms of geographic boundaries, and shift our thinking to include the digital mission field.

Don't leave it up to IT or the tech team to manage your social media channels. This responsibility needs to be led by someone with communication and customer service skills. Most organizations wouldn't send an intern or IT person to respond to a PR crisis or media inquiry, yet it happens online with little to no guidance more often than we'd like to admit.

Dawn Nicole Baldwin
Brand Strategist

As an example of the influence potential of social media, at the time I'm writing this, I have more than 17,000 followers of my Twitter account, and growing. In a way, that makes me the pastor of one of the largest churches in America. That means I'm potentially influencing significant numbers of people on a daily basis.

But that's nothing to brag about. I spoke at a leadership event recently with football player Tim Tebow, who has almost 2 million Twitter followers.

What makes this powerful is not necessarily the number of eyes who potentially read my tweets (and I certainly don't think all of them do). It is the fact that many people can very easily take my words and integrate them into *their* story. They can comment about my tweet and re-tweet it to their own followers, which will start a conversation with me that I would never have had otherwise. That conversation can then be seen and continued among their followers and friends.

Mark Dreisdadt, founder and CEO of the advertising and marketing firm Infinity Concepts, says, "To consider whether or not to invest in social media is much like deciding whether or not to invest in a phone system. Neither tool provides a direct return on investment, but without either tool, any return on investment will be greatly diminished." There are too many people connecting their stories on social media platforms to be ignored, especially if you have the good news of your story and brand to share with them and you want them to participate in it with you.

Vimeo (vī/mēo) and **YouTube** (yü/tüb): These are video-based social media sites where users can upload video content that they've created, whether it's a professional short film or a clip of a giant panda sneezing (that actually was a popular one for a while). Users can comment on each other's videos or post the URL for a particular video to their own Facebook, Twitter or blog. The big deal here is about gaining popularity by racking up the total number of views. Some videos have been viewed millions of times and are competing with network TV for viewers.

Three Qualities About Social Media that Humans Value

Why do so many people use social media? While Facebook and Twitter are all the buzz these days, they continue to grow not just because of their popularity. In fact, Facebook and Twitter could fade out as fast as their predecessors. At one point, MySpace, the former king of social media, sold to News Corp for $580 million. A few years later, they were lucky to dump it for $35 million. Social media platforms like Facebook and Twitter may just as easily go away, but the use of technology and the Internet to socialize and connect with others will not. That's because at the heart of social media are three important qualities we value in the human experience.[8]

> Because so many people are including us in their personal story via Twitter, I don't have to write informational tweets. Instead of tweeting "Join us for Celebrate Recovery tonight at 7:30 PM," I retweet the volunteer who says, "Praying for CR tonight, can't wait to take another step toward freedom. Join me tonight at 7 PM @OasisLA." We have hundreds of brand ambassadors sharing our story for us.
>
> **Kristen Tarsiuk**
> Communications Director, Oasis Church in Los Angeles

1. Connectedness

Human beings crave connection with other people and with the world around them. We strive to know other people and be known by them. We feel more connected when we read their everyday thoughts. Even better, we like the option to comment on those everyday thoughts in order to share our own thoughts and reactions. The interchange of ideas, emotions, prayers and memories over social media builds connection. As Kristen Tarsiuk, the communications director of Oasis Church in Los Angeles, points out, this connection is a *supplement* not a *substitute* for in-person connectivity. The Facebook-to-Facebook connection can't replace the face-to-face interactions we have. But it can help strengthen them.

Social media users also value connectedness with the world around them. The issues about which other users bookmark, post, blog or tweet connect us to issues that normally we may never see. Even if I read most of the daily newspapers and websites, I may never hear about some topics that don't make it into the mainstream media. Social media opens connections beyond just the *people* to the world around those people, ultimately networking all corners of the world closer together.

Transparency is key in social media. Churches, ministries, and nonprofits have an opportunity in social media to set themselves apart from everyone else. Be real. Be transparent. Social media gives you an incredible opportunity.

Brian Boyd
CEO and Founder of Media Connect Partners

Ironically, while we desperately desire connection, we also greatly fear it. Desire for connection and fear of it are what make social networking so appealing. It provides a sense of connection, yet it allows enough control so that we get to influence how much people see of us. In 2011, Mark Zuckerberg posted a long letter on Facebook's blog to emphasize how important this control was to him from the beginning. At the time he wrote the blog, Facebook had been blasted by critics for new control settings that took away users' control of their privacy. Zuckerberg responded by pointing out that users' individual control of what they shared was what made Facebook successful. People want to be connected, but they want to do it on their own terms.

2. Transparency

This second value may seem ironic in light of what I just said about controlling what level of information we share. However, spend only a short time surfing through a few users' profiles and you may be surprised at what information they offer. They'll comment about every mundane event of their day, from their boring day at work to changing their kid's diaper. They'll post angry reviews of presidential speeches they just heard or mean comments about people (about those they know personally and those they don't). They'll have photos of themselves at events where there's clearly illegal activity going on around them. In fact, I know of numerous pastors who nearly lost their jobs because of an online comment or video that revealed a brief moment where they appeared to be doing something particularly insensitive or outright stupid.

> Reviews and feedback matter. Organizations need to create the structure to know if someone who attended a single service or event and produced a negative review so that you can contact them and try to resolve the issue before thousands of people read it. That could be a great thing or a nightmare depending on how the organization handles it. Using social media to monitor your reputation is the new normal; fail to do so at your own risk.
>
> **Brad Davies**
> Director of Web Services, Dunham+Company

People are transparent through social media even in ways they don't intend. By tracking what kinds of news articles a person regularly tags and comments about, you can learn a lot about his or her political, religious and personal views. You can also do this by looking at what companies or activities a person says they "like" in their personal profile. A number of companies count on this kind of information in order to customize their advertising. One particular company tried to find celebrities who would endorse a nonprofit organization that advocated for better schools in America. The company searched through past tweets of major celebrities to find which ones made the most comments about the American school system. The strategy worked. They found the right celebrities, who ended up endorsing the nonprofit.

The ability of the Internet, mobile, financial and other companies to make sense of all of this aggregated information should be a wake-up call for the Church. As my friend Leonard Sweet wrote in his book *Viral: How Social Networking Is Poised to Ignite Revival*, "Marissa Mayer, a Google vice-president, boasts that credit card companies can predict with 98 percent accuracy two years in advance when a couple is going to divorce, based on the couple's spending patterns."[9]

While we may be slightly scared of this much transparency, social media users love it when it comes to their friends or issues they're interested in. I'll get a request to become friends on Facebook with someone I haven't seen since high school; and one of the first things I'll do is look at recent photos of them. Where have they been? What are they up to? Have they had a facelift? Social media transparency has also blown the covers off many hot-button political issues—economic injustices, politicians posting lewd photos, and the like. With an international user base, people in America can see a post about a riot in Europe on Twitter before the news can even report it. We value transparency like this for the positive impact it has on our lives, even if it can deeply wound us someday.

The upside of "transparency" as it relates to the message of the gospel is *authenticity*. This generation is far more likely to trust a friend's recommendation via social media than your local billboard or banner ad. Churches that are used to controlling a one-way conversation when it comes to sharing their story are in for trouble in the social media world. But if you thrive on being open and honest, social media can be a great asset.

3. Immediacy

Social media further allows for an immediacy of information and human interaction. When close friends are going through big events in their lives, we don't have to wait to hear the news. We want the information as quickly as possible. So, if a couple gives birth to a baby, they can take a photo of the newborn swaddled in pink or blue and post it online or have a friend "live-blogging" from the waiting room as it happens. If a close friend was hurt in a car crash, I could follow his condition through updates his family provides through social networking sites.

Social media allows for immediacy beyond our close circle of family and friends, as well. Twitter and other social networking sites allow for real-time searches for information. With so many users, people who use social media will comment about an event before most major sites can write about it. Even if the major sites didn't release an article about the event, a Google search would have to wait for the major site to get enough viewers before the Google search engine would recognize its popularity and show it to me. But with social media, I can do a search of the posts and tweets people have made and usually come up with an answer far before a Google search would show me. For example, when a crisis happens anywhere in the world, I'll probably notice it on Twitter first. I'll find answers in real time far quicker than other search engines.

The immediacy of social media allows users to get to quality information faster than ever before. This may hurt us by shaping us into people who expect the world to be at our digital fingertips. Still, great benefits come with the ability to quickly communicate with one another.

Maybe you already understand how effective social media is, but you're struggling with getting the rest of the people around you to come onboard. I would say, start here, with the core qualities of human relationship that people find in social media. More than just these three values exist, so spend time with your team exploring what the audience truly values in this technology. When you and your team can connect your personal values with those of the multitudes on social media platforms, the "goodness" of what this means for connection will become more evident. The question will then move from *why* should you take your brand on social media to *how* can you do it with the greatest impact.

Flickr (fli/kər) and **Instagram** (in/sta/gram): These are image-hosting websitses and online community platforms. In addition to being popular sites for users to share personal photographs, the Flickr service is widely used by bloggers as a photo repository they link to from articles on their blogs.

It's Time to Get into the Pool

The key to effectively engaging an audience with your brand through social media means initiating the interaction you want to have with your audience and then *responding* to them. The biggest mistake people make is thinking that having a social media *presence* will inherently build a solid connection between people and their brand.

Picture that you're new to the neighborhood and you go to a party in hopes of connecting with many new friends. When you show up, you just stand in the corner. You probably can already tell this scenario is not going to help you meet people. Even if someone *does* happen to venture over to you, there won't be any connection after they leave if you just stay in the corner. Setting up a Facebook page or Twitter account, or writing a blog, is the equivalent to just *showing up* at the party. If you want to form a real connection, you have to get out of the corner and initiate interaction with others.

The great thing about social media is that both party-lovers and party-avoiders can utilize it. The platforms are universal enough to include you whether you can only give it 15 minutes a day or are hired as a company's social media manager. But on either end of the spectrum, you need to participate by reaching out to others.

As social media consultant Brian Boyd, CEO and founder of Media Connect Partners, has said, "Here are two ways to fail with your social media plan: (1) lack of fresh original content, and (2) failure to listen and interact. When someone makes a comment—positive or negative—on your social platforms, get in the conversation!"

Making the Most of Social Media

Dawn Nicole Baldwin, Branding Strategist at AspireOne, uses an excellent checklist to help develop an initial social media strategy.

Define the Purpose
What are you primarily hoping to accomplish? How will you measure success? Quick examples:

1. Size of community/number of followers
2. Ability to motivate the group (rally around a cause)
3. Number of comments or interactions
4. Number of invitations to speak at conferences, events and so on as a subject "expert"

What is measured is typically what succeeds, so you need to be intentional with your efforts.

Understand Your Audience
What types of people are most interested in what you have to say? Why? What is important to them? What similar topics (besides your organization) might they also be interested in? Having a clear picture of whom you are connecting with and why will enable you to tailor your content so that it's more effective.

Be a Good Host
View each channel as a group of new and potential friends that are coming to your house for a gathering. Don't blast information about your products or services all the time. A 10:1 ratio is a good rule of thumb. Share or promote content about others 10 times for every 1 time you promote yourself. (Stories in the field don't

count as products or services.) The key is to engage, so be sure to respond to questions and comments. A 24-hour turnaround is viewed as acceptable. Days or weeks without a response (or none at all) isn't okay.

A Quick List of Social Media Dos and Don'ts:
Dawn Nicole Baldwin's list of dos and don'ts is a great reminder, especially for social media novices:

1. Don't treat social media the same as other communication efforts. View it as a community, and build a relationship first.

2. Don't try to do everything at once. Bite off little pieces at a time and ensure that it's being done well to avoid feeling overwhelmed. It's better to not have a presence in every channel than one that is ineffective, neglected or mismanaged.

3. Don't freak out over every negative comment. If it's a one-off remark, decide if it's worth responding to or not. (This is where your friends and fans can come to your defense as well.)

4. Don't "sanitize" your channels by removing any/all negative comments. This seems like the organization has something to hide, and it doesn't feel authentic. Transparency is key for social media.

5. Do be intentional about the tone of your response. Getting defensive or allowing a hint of hostility to sneak in just makes you and your organization look bad. Do have goals established of what needs to be accomplished as a whole and with each channel.

6. Do have an idea of how success will be measured. Above all, view this as a strategic channel to build a relationship with your audience.

Who Exactly Is Your Audience?

You can start your initiation by first listening to the different social media platforms. Do your research beyond mere statistics. Ask people who use social media platforms why they use them, what they like and what they don't like about them. Try to get a sense for the values in the social media community. What you'll come to find is that there are particular kinds of people who use one platform over another. Some of the most adept users of social media will have a Facebook account but won't have a Twitter account, or vice versa. Why is that?

In my personal experience, I find that Twitter users tend to be more of a professional nature. They like the quick, neat, streamlined thoughts they can share and hear from others. For instance, when I post a comment to Twitter, with some exceptions, I generally get back serious, professional comments and questions. But the same post to Facebook elicits a long string of college dorm humor. Different platforms, different personalities. If you dig around enough and pay attention, you'll find this general sense of audience across the board, which will inform you on how to best utilize each platform.

Geo-locating (jēo/lō/kāt/iŋ): How social media platforms use a person's current location to let other users know where they are or allow the user to see businesses in their vicinity and even get coupon offers from those businesses.

To really explore these audiences, you'll have to dive right in. Start simple by setting up an account on one or two platforms at first. Maybe try two different forms of social networking sites, like Facebook and Google+. Or try a Twitter account and a blog. Give each 15 minutes a day and build a habit of posting your own material and interacting with other people.

By the way, *interacting* is the key. I said earlier that social media is *social*, which means that you don't just update your status or write a post. You read how other people are responding to *you* and then you respond to *them*. Think of it as a conversation, not a lecture.

Another important issue to remember is that there are apps that take your Twitter post and automatically make it your Facebook status update. Other apps go the opposite direction—FB update to Twitter post. While each audience deserves it's own messaging, the fact is that if you're a leader, you have other things to do than update your Facebook page all day. So don't be afraid to streamline the process.

There's no shame in social media convenience.

What Should You Post?

Remember that your social media presence is an extension of your personal brand. So go back to the four key questions that help define your story and do your best to stay in that lane. Obviously, you can post both personal and professional comments, but if you want to stand out in your niche—your *one big thing*—then use your social media platforms to extend that message.

Post about issues that matter to you. Try posting a news article you've recently read. Write a quote you've been pondering recently. Even try putting a provocative question out there without giving your opinion.

Here are my own personal priorities when it comes to my Twitter/Facebook posts:

1. Give People an Intimate Look at What It's Like to Be You

People don't care that you're eating a ham sandwich or have just walked into the grocery store. To a great extent, people follow you to learn about your life and your story. What are your struggles? What are your concerns? Your victories? I often encourage pastors to share what they're wrestling with on Saturday night as they agonize over the next day's sermon. Perhaps you can share the thoughts running through your mind as you prepare to conduct the funeral of someone in your congregation. What about the frustration of raising funds for an important outreach in a Third World country, or your idea for launching a new homeless ministry?

Want to see your social media followers grow? Give them a look behind the scenes of your life and ministry. If you're a filmmaker, writer or artist, tell them about that brainstorm that's sparking your new project. Or tell them about the tough day pitching that project to investors or a studio. Open up.

The bottom line: Give them the inside story that they can't find elsewhere.

2. Be Provocative

I like to toss out the occasional hand grenade. I'm not big on gratuitous or silly controversy, but I love a great, animated discussion. Upset the applecart. As in the title of one of my books, give people a *Jolt!* Shake up their thinking. Jesus was brilliant at shattering preconceived ideas and busting silos. In your area of expertise or brand, what are the issues that need to be rethought? Challenge people's thinking, and you'll start a very interesting string of online conversations.

Provoking conversation that isn't run-of-the-mill thinking is one of the most effective ways to stand out.

3. Be Encouraging

People live challenging lives and need that occasional dose of encouragement. But let me be clear: If I get another Twitter post, email or Facebook update with another cheesy poem, tear-jerking story or cat video, I'm going to shoot someone. And if you tell me, "If you love Jesus, resend this to all your friends," I'm coming to your house, and it's not going to be pretty. I'm pretty sure I'm not the only person who feels this way. So be honest and real. Stop resending other people's cornball stuff and encourage others in a way that gets their attention and makes them stop in their tracks.

Make them think.

4. There's Power in Great Quotes

When I come across a great quote in my reading, I'll write "Twitter" in the margin of the magazine or book and post it later. Share your great finds. Let people know what brilliant quotes you come across. Don't hesitate to share what you've found meaningful in your reading, devotions or the notes you've taken from great speakers. Don't steal, but share what you think is important. It adds to your credibility.

Relationship should always come before opportunity. Churches and nonprofits have a clear mission but are also made up of real people that want to be cared about and not pushed and sold. Having a good strategy and clear purpose is crucial, but it needs to be paired with a relational approach. Those succeeding with social media understand that being "human" and "genuine" is vital.

Sean Cannell
Think International

As you try different types of posts, pay attention to how people interact with you. This will help you learn how to make more effective posts and respond to the personalities and concerns of your followers and, yes, "fans." Look at what time of day people respond the most. It may be that you make the strongest connection with people when they're on their lunch break. So post more during that time or make sure you make yourself available to respond to others in real time. Check out what posts are most effective at particular times of the day or around certain holidays. It could be that mornings and the Christmas season are times when people want to read uplifting stories and see happy photos. Change your posting habits for these and other factors.

I live in Los Angeles, so for me, I get the most responses when I post from 9:00 AM to 3:00 PM Pacific Standard Time. Before 9:00 AM,

West Coast people aren't really connecting online; and after 3:00 PM PST, East Coast people appear to have tuned out. Certainly, a great number of people check their social media pages later in the evening, so see if that time resonates with your connections. Because I speak and teach internationally, I also will use apps that allow me to schedule my posts so my friends in Europe, Africa or Asia can be part of the conversation.

Check that out. You may be more popular in Indonesia than you are in your hometown.

Social bookmarking (sō/shəl/buk/märk/iŋ): refers to platforms that allow users to "bookmark" what websites they have been reading. A popular example of this is Digg.com, which will tell a user the top websites other users "Digg" on the Internet. This form of social media is reshaping how people receive their news by having them read articles based on user-voted-popularity rather than by location like traditional news sources.

If you're a large organization with a Facebook "fan" page, you also have access to Facebook Insights. Insights will give you statistical information about your posts and friends, such as age demographics or region of the world. You can make your posts specific to an audience in a particular region if you, for example, know you're going to travel to that area soon.

There's no exact science to posting. Sometimes I'll post something that I think is staggering genius, but it drops like a brick. The social media silence can be deafening. Other times, I'll post something silly and inconsequential, but it explodes across multiple platforms.

How Do You Find an Audience?

In order for people to know that you and your brand exist, you have to request them as friends (on Facebook), follow their tweets (on Twitter), comment on their blogs, and simply get your name out there. Start by looking for people and larger organizations that have similarities to you and your brand. If you run a company that makes the best darn pies in the state, search for other bakers, restaurants, food lovers, and sweet-tooth folk. Begin a conversation with them, because a number of things could happen. They now have you in their mental "rolodex" (remember that word?) under Best Darn Pies. Their friends/followers are going to see your comments, which makes them more likely to interact with you. And best of all, you'll generate interest in your own Darn Good Pies so that people will come to you to have a conversation about the Best Darn Pies in the State.

What all this interaction is leading toward is your brand/story becoming a part of other people's stories—and most important, connecting to the focus of your life, career or ministry. This is when your brand takes off like wildfire. The best thing you can ask for is when people start talking about you and your brand when you're not even at the party.

Few organizations and companies reach this level. Apple is a good example of one that has. Apple fans talk about their Apple products on their social media platforms—*a lot*. Even if you're not selling a product but are just inviting people into a cause, or your religious community, you want to aid people in the process of interweaving their story with yours in the hope they'll share it with friends.

As Kristen Tarsiuk puts it, you want to empower *brand ambassadors*. Say you have an event coming up on a particular date in the near future. You could keep making your own posts telling people about it. But the better choice is if a volunteer from your event comments about it, then you comment on their post or re-tweet their comment. In the social media world, "RT" next to someone's post means that the tweet was originally written by someone else and then re-tweeted. Doing this supports people's integration of your brand into their own stories, while it also tells others that there are people interested in *you*. Studies actually suggest that the more that people see greater numbers following and commenting about you, the greater they perceive your credibility.[10]

Here's one of my favorite examples of reaching out to a fan. A high school girl was participating in a sporting event when afterward she found her sandals had been stolen. She made a tweet about the sandals being stolen and mentioned the sandal manufacturer's name in her tweet. The social media director of the sandal company saw the girl's tweet because the company name was mentioned. Without the girl even asking for it, the social media director sent her a free, new pair of sandals. You can bet that girl then posted it on all her social media platforms. Simple as that, the sandal company became part of the girl's story, which then stretched into others' stories; and now it is here in your copy of this book.

When Friends/Followers/Reviewers Aren't So Nice

The most challenging part of social media is that it fully exposes you and your brand to opinions you often can't control. Keep in mind that engaging in the Internet means that you lose control of your brand. You can certainly *influence* it, but you can't *control* it.

Amidst the "likes" and positive reviews you'll receive, I can guarantee at least a few people won't like what you're doing. In the old days, if a customer, visitor or donor had a bad experience, they would tell six of their friends. But in a social media universe, when that customer, visitor or donor has a bad experience, they can tell *6,000* of their friends. Because of social media, that one person also comes with a megaphone. Based on how you handle the situation, however, this could work to your benefit.

Listen to the critic and figure out if he or she has a legitimate concern. Check to see if there's something you can learn. Maybe it will show you how to conduct your parking lot better or how to welcome first-time guests to your church or events. Be open to the fact that maybe you communicated something that really hurt this person. Say that you're a pastor and you deliver a particularly difficult sermon on a controversial subject. Through social media, you have a chance to look through the profiles and history of your toughest critics. In that, you may find they've been hurt in their past.

At the same time, have a strategy in place for how to handle rude criticism that carries on too long, that is really off the mark or is crude and destructive to others. Recently, a major airline discovered an extremely vocal critic on Twitter. Because their social media manager was watching the feed very closely, the disgruntled person was noticed pretty quickly. The social media manager immediately responded on Twitter, noted the person's frustration and gave him an email address so that he could go offline and be dealt with directly.

Notice three things:

1. The company immediately responded. They didn't wait for it to fester or go viral. By monitoring their social media traffic, they spotted the critic almost immediately.

2. They took him offline. They got him out of the public stream and immediately took the criticism off the radar and quieted the critic's voice.

3. They solved his problem. By giving him an email address, it allowed him to voice his frustration, and they worked to solve his problem. In the end, he became a loyal customer.

How could that strategy minimize the criticism of your organization?

Understand that it's okay to ask a critic who has made a negative post about you or your brand to carry the conversation to a less public forum. Communicate with them by email or phone and, in certain cases, as long as it doesn't endanger you, try to meet with them in person.

Streaming (strē-miŋ) and **progressive downloads** (prə/gre/siv/daun/lōds): These refer to methods by which media content (usually video or audio) is streamed/downloaded from a host website to a user's individual computer. Forgive me if I've left out your favorite site in these social media definitions, but I could go on forever, and this is enough to paint the big picture. Dozens more websites fall into the category of social media, but the ones defined in this chapter are currently some of the major players.

The ultimate goal of social media is this genuine, person-to-person relationship. Social media serves as a conversation starter between your story and the stories of others. What you want is for that conversation to invite people to participate in developing your brand, your story. You want, no, you *need* them to become living bodies in your life. From the stingiest of for-profit businesses to the smallest of churches, the physical presence of a person far outweighs the digital version of him or her. What good are a few posts if they don't lead to bodies entering into your community, or store? At the end of the day, people matter most, not their "likes" or RT. As much as possible, you want to share the good news of your brand with people in person.

Can you imagine doing ministry the last five hundred years and getting away with "Sorry, I don't do books"? Can you imagine doing ministry in the next five years and getting away with "Sorry, I don't do Facebook"?

Leonard Sweet
Writer and Social Critic

The Gospel of Social Media

Remember what I said in the opening to this chapter? A brand survives based on the goodness it offers, and it grows based on how well that goodness interacts with people's lives. Facebook, Twitter, Pinterest or other platforms will come and go. In fact, some of the major sites may be gone by the time you read this book. But social media is surviving (and will continue to survive in some form or another) because it's built around something that is good—*human connection*. Theologians, philosophers, psychologists and social critics can judge the quality of that connection all they want. But human connection is so critical in its essence that even the *digital* form found in social media is worthwhile. The gospel of social media grows because as more people gain access to the Internet, they are able to interact with the goodness found in social media—the human connection.

Social media has a gospel, and it's growing and reshaping by the minute. So I encourage you to start today to find how you can share the gospel of your brand in this growing—no, *explosively* growing—area.

Some final social media thoughts:

• Encourage volunteers (of your nonprofit) or members (of your church) or clients and customers (of your business) to make comments online. Have them share their experiences of your product, service or cause with their friends. Staff and employees should do it as well, but nonstaff members tend to paint more honest pictures.

• Check online reviews regularly. Outside of Facebook and Twitter, people will write reviews about you on Yelp.com, Google and other popular sites. Listen to the reviews, learn from them, respond to them; but don't get obsessive.

• Rather than focusing just on your company, organization or church's Facebook/Twitter account, encourage your leaders and staff to have their own personal profiles. People connect to other people better than they do to institutional pages.

• If you're not comfortable with social media, don't feel bad about that. Just don't do it. I'd rather you not get into the pool at all than drown. The last thing we need is another well-intentioned but really bad witness. Relax. If you're not comfortable with it, don't do it.

However, you were interested enough to read this book, right?

Take Your **Thinking Deeper**

1. What are you doing right now on social media? Are you using it primarily as a tool to speak just to personal family and friends, or are you developing it as a strategy to share your story on a much bigger scale?

2. Is your social media "social"? Are you *responding* to the people who are engaging with you?

3. What social media platforms . . .

   • are you using most effectively?
   • are you most comfortable using?
   • is your potential audience using?

4. A blog is a potentially powerful way to develop a following of people interested in what you have to say. Should you be blogging? Before you answer that, here are a few questions:

   • Do you love to write?
   • Do you have something to say?
   • Could you focus on your niche or area of expertise?
   • Can you be transparent and authentic, rather than promotional?
   • Can you produce a few paragraphs at least three times a week?

5. In social media, what do you want to accomplish? What will success look like for you? Do you know the audience you're trying to reach?

Aesthetics, or styling, has become an accepted unique selling point—on a global basis. In a crowded marketplace, aesthetics is often the only way to make a product stand out.

Virginia Postral

The Substance of Style[1]

Great Design

The Language of a Generation

Governments, dictators, business leaders and global influencers of all kinds have spent centuries trying to discover how to bring together organizations, communities and nations. Time and time again, they've found one answer.

Design.

Early in the life of the Church, the Christian community discovered the transforming power of images. From Byzantine paintings and mosaics to the great art of the Middle Ages and Renaissance, and the icons of Eastern Orthodoxy, the Church presented its message through the narrative storytelling of images. Under Communism, Lenin exploited the influence of propaganda posters, and it didn't take long for the kings of American business to investigate the visual power of advertising. For good or bad, since the earliest days of recorded history, the power of design has influenced millions.

And now, once again, design has united a generation.

From the intense graphic design of video games to the pioneering special effects of major motion pictures; from the storyboards of music videos and commercials to high-definition television, young people today speak the language of design. Kids today can retouch digital photos while in elementary school; and by middle school, they are accomplished Web designers.

> **We live in a design-driven generation,**
> **and if the Church is going to make an impact,**
> **design is the language we must learn.**

In Western culture, content has always been king. From the early days of the Hebrew Scriptures to the spread of Christianity across Western Europe and eventually America, we've been a word-based people. William Tyndale's translation of the Bible into English sparked a revolution of literacy in the sixteenth century; and the greatest missionary efforts of the last few centuries have been the goals of translating and distributing the biblical text to every culture and people group on the planet.

Kathleen and I have begun collecting rare Bibles. Our collection is very modest, but it's an amazing thing to hold a Bible in your hand that was printed before the first settlers stepped off the ship onto North American soil. Seeing the extreme care that went into the earliest printed Bibles has made me realize just how much people of that time valued the written word.

As a result—and rightly so—content has been far more important than form in most expressions of our faith. But today, we live in a design culture, and form has become a critical key to connecting with the public. So while biblical literacy can never be taken for granted, we now face a new challenge: presenting a message of hope to a generation that's more visually sophisticated than any generation in history.

I call design *the language of this generation*; although many have criticized the transition of the faith from a text-based culture, we have to realize the change that is happening right now and respond with vigor. In a typical church or nonprofit setting, here are some simple places where strong design can make a difference:

- Print advertising
- Logo design
- Product packaging
- Business cards and stationery
- Electronic or printed church or ministry newsletters
- Websites
- Email "blasts" to members, partners and supporters
- Event flyers and invitations
- Social media page design
- Press releases and electronic press kits
- Posters
- Church program brochures
- Thank-you notes
- Church or ministry facility signage
- Architectural and interior design
- Banners
- Television and video programming
- Sermon or teaching series branding
- Image magnification
- Church video announcements

There are many more options, but that should give you an idea why talented graphic artists are one of the most coveted employees churches and ministries can find.

Another alternative is finding a graphic design company on the outside and using them for the major projects or to help you design a production style guide to show your in-house graphics team how to use the logo and branding most effectively and appropriately.

In the secular world, major companies are very strict about using their logo designs. Early in my career, I was asked to write and produce a short film for a major oil company in the wake of a disastrous explosion at one of their refineries, causing multiple deaths and hundreds of millions of dollars in damage. The purpose of the video was to document the rebuilding of the refinery and to show their sensitivity to the environment and to families of the deceased.

During the editing phase of the project, I was presented with a 40-page "style guide" that indicated in very precise terms the exact usage of the company's logo and color scheme. In addition, they dispatched a company attorney to sit in the editing suite to verify that I was using the logo correctly. That was a company that realized the power of their corporate brand and wanted to make sure their identity was very carefully presented to the pubic.

In the book *Branding for Non-Profits: Developing Identity with Integrity*, D. K. Holland asks these key questions during the design phase of a branding project:

- How valid is the concept for the organization?
- How powerful is the concept? Will our primary audiences connect to it on an emotional level?
- How original is the concept? Can we "own" this concept, or is it too generic?
- Is the concept clear and focused, or is it ambiguous? Can it be interpreted in more ways than one? If so, does it support our cause, or undermine it?
- Is the concept versatile, or rigid? Does it have legs—in other words, is it flexible enough to be used in a variety of ways that build a brand with depth?
- Can the logo be reduced or enlarged and still maintain its integrity? Can it be used in black and white and remain legible?[2]

A Logo Isn't a Brand

It's important to remember that a logo is not a brand; it's the visual expression of the brand and reflects the DNA of the brand. Most churches and ministries get hung up on the logo, but I never bring in the graphic artist until we've very carefully created the brand story we want to tell. At that point, the artist can help us design a logo that expresses that story to the public.

Beginning today . . .
symbols will be replacing words.
Jodi Bernstein
Director, FTC Bureau of Consumer Protection

The key is to share your brand story with the artist and provide enough information about you and your organization. If you've hired a talented designer, then let him (or her) do his job. Although you should feel free to share any ideas you have, let the designer have the artistic freedom to experiment and try some new approaches.

Some artists like to present you with 10 to 20 or more sketches; others prefer 2 to 3 sketches. Some like rough pencil sketches, and others like to only show clients finished work. Whatever style the designer prefers, discuss it beforehand and make sure you both understand the parameters, the budget and the expectations.

The evidence for great design is everywhere. Just check out the unique design features of new computers or the interior design of coffee shops. Cell phones, automobiles, software, movies—even office chairs—all are examples of a design-driven culture. Better design isn't just decoration; it's connection. Iconic designer Charles Eames said, "Design is a plan for action."

Sure, sixteenth-century Pope Julius II could have had the ceiling of the Vatican's Sistine Chapel painted a nice solid color, but he chose to give Michelangelo a little creative challenge. We Christians should have learned something by that, but today we build churches in metal buildings, design boring websites and create tacky covers and product packaging.

Nearly 100 percent of potential visitors
today will check out your website before they visit
your church. So why is your website so lame?

As a producer and media consultant, I have spent decades encouraging clients to realize the power of design to connect with
customers, and recognize its influence on getting a message heard.
I recommend that churches and ministries reconsider worship
graphics and images, product packaging, television programming,
websites, publications—anything they create—with a new attitude
toward design. Rethinking the design elements of a project isn't
just a cosmetic issue; it's a fundamental issue about something
that connects with the audience or customer on a very deep and
significant level.

Don't toss out your Bibles, commentaries or reference books.
The power of text will always be critical in telling the eternal story
of our faith experience. But without a visual element to your
brand, reaching this generation will prove far more difficult than
you could possibly imagine. Creating a ministry outreach that
presents the gospel in a compelling way that will capture the hearts
and minds of the mainstream audience is difficult enough; but a
sure ticket into the mindshare of young people is the power of
graphic design and visuals.

Great design inspires passion.

Brand Unity

The need for good design happens on a number of levels. First,
you establish a strong and evocative logo, which then dictates the
visual style of your print look and feel. Second, you create a style
guide—usually created by a designer—that details how the new
logo, color scheme and style should be used throughout the ministry. This will allow your in-house production artists to understand how to use the new style effectively and not undermine the
new visual identity.

Third, the good, strong design creates brand unity, which is the act of unifying all visual outreaches of the ministry so that no matter how someone comes in contact with the church or ministry, they experience the same look and feel.

There are various ministry touch points where customers, church members or supporters may come in contact with the organization:

- Television
- Website
- Brochures and other printed material
- Email notices and blasts
- Business stationery—cards, letterhead, envelopes
- Banners or posters
- Social media sites
- Book covers
- Product packaging
- Print advertisements in various magazines and newspapers

One of the greatest challenges I face when working with churches and ministries is that most of the time all these products look different. In some cases, the variations are so great that each product looks like it was produced by a different organization. We worked with one church that had 60 different logos for various outreaches of the church!

In a media-driven culture filled with advertising clutter, impressions are critical in getting a message across. I'm so busy during a typical day that when something really important comes up, my assistant will often tell me about it, remind me later, send a follow-up email, put it on my calendar and then add it to my to-do list. Critical messages need to punch through the clutter of all the other issues fighting for my attention.

Your viewers and supporters are experiencing the same type of clutter; if multiple impressions do not tell the same story and message, your communication just won't get through.

Brand unity helps make sure the message hits the target by telling the same brand story throughout any touch point your audience might encounter. The message they receive at church supports the visual message they receive in the mail, see on television or encounter on your website. Instead of different visual messages hitting like scattershot, your audience is on the receiving end of a laser beam, receiving your communication with much greater intensity and power.

I can't stress enough the importance of brand unity because of its ultimate impact on the success and effectiveness of your outreach.

Take Your **Thinking Deeper**

1. Take a hard look at the designs that surround you and your organization. What do you see and think? Are they contemporary, high quality and meaningful? Or out of date and out of touch?

2. What about brand unity? If you spread out all your brochures, the look of your websites, product packaging and other design-driven pieces—do they all reflect the same story and style? Or could they come from a number of different organizations?

3. Is your logo up to date, and does it express your brand story well? Remember: A logo isn't your brand; a logo is the visual expression of your brand. With that in mind, how does your logo stack up?

4. What will a potential visitor or customer find when he or she visits your website for the first time? Is it easy for a visitor to find what he or she wants? Is it visually interesting and simple to navigate? Is there a reason to come back?

5. What about the design of your social media pages? Do they look the same as everyone else's, or do yours stand out?

6. Think about all the ways that good design can help support your message, share your story and help people connect more effectively and successfully with your organization.

> He who marries the spirit of the age soon becomes a widower. As with great art, faith that lasts is faith that answers to higher standards than today's trends.
>
> **Dean Inge**
> St. Paul's Cathedral in London

The Dark Side of Branding

The Digital Revolution, Chasing Relevance and the Marketing Conflict

The entire concept of branding often raises such a red flag for Christian believers that I rarely have a conversation about the subject without a debate (often quite lively) about the negative connotations of branding as well. For a multitude of reasons, branding and its close relative, marketing, have gotten a bad reputation in the church, probably as much for its inept execution than anything else. But there are several strong reasons why I continue to keep the dialogue going about branding's relevance to churches, ministries and other nonprofits.

Like most areas of life, the greatest dangers often come out of the strongest positives; so, like a two-edged sword, we need to closely examine all aspects of branding. Through my own experience, I've discovered that the three most dangerous areas of branding are (1) technology, (2) chasing relevance, and (3) a key conflict with the concept of marketing.

It has become appallingly obvious that our technology has exceeded our humanity.
Albert Einstein

The Dangers of the Digital Revolution

It would be a profound mistake to realize the possibilities of telling the right brand story about you, your church or your ministry without also understanding that, like most media issues, branding can have unintended consequences and sometimes seriously negative implications for the culture. From what I call the "pornographication" of our culture through the sexualizing of nearly everything, to the loss of community, digital technology has implications that we have yet to fully understand.

Mercer Schuchardt captured the concern very well in an online post on theooze.com:

> If sport is the religion of the modern age, then Nike has successfully become the official church. It is a church whose icon serves as an allegory that formulates salvation in a special parabolical and symbolic language. The Swoosh is a window on the border between this world and the other, between your existing self (you overweight slob) and your Nike self (you god of fitness), where salvation is the attainment of the athletic Nietzschean ideal: no fear, no mercy, no second place. The Swoosh is a true religious icon in that it serves as a representation of the reality and as a participant in the reality; you do, after all, have to wear

something to attain this special salvation, so why not something emblazoned with that Swoosh?

How powerful is the zeal spawned by the cult of Nike? So powerful, that we kill for it. Since 1991, five Americans have been shot to death for the Nikes on their feet. Lt. Thomas Malacek, the officer handling one of the cases, said, "It's becoming a growing problem, because apparently these items have a lot more identity value than in the past."

Well, you say, the kids are crazy these days, and there's a whole slew of other factors involved in each one of these deaths: Poverty. Race. Violence. Family breakdown.

Sure, but it still begs the question: How come no one's ever died for a pair of Reeboks?

Or Adidas?

Or Filas?[1]

As I've mentioned before, some branding critics have pointed to the sweatshops of the Third World, mass producing tennis shoes, the pollution created by factories, or even the globalization of the economy. While those issues are all serious, I don't see them as a result of the rise in global branding and marketing. Certainly sweatshops existed long before American companies started manufacturing tennis shoes; unsafe factories were killing people in the nineteenth century, and globalization has always been the inevitable result of expanding markets.

Global corporations are in business to make money, and in a secular society, many do whatever it takes. Using branding as well as a multitude of other business and marketing tools, they're going to wreak havoc on local economies, child labor laws, pollution guidelines, and more. But we don't stop using good accounting principles because of the bookkeeping abuses of Enron; and we don't stop investing because Bernard Madoff admitted to operating a Ponzi scheme considered to be the largest financial fraud in American history.

We live in a horribly fallen world, but that doesn't excuse us from making our voice heard in the public square and trying to change the culture. As Christians, we have the highest responsibility toward our fellow man, Christian and non-Christian alike, and should be working to make sure that technology serves the public good.

My personal concerns about the negative implications of digital media and branding revolve around our sense of community and space—how it affects our personal relationships and changes our behavior.

In the first chapter, I mentioned the *Los Angeles Times* newspaper story reporting on cell phone use in Korea that revealed remarkable information about where our digital culture may be heading. They discovered that Korean teenagers make up to 90 cell phone calls a day, and social scientists are now beginning to correlate high cell use with rising rates of depression in that country. Here at home, I've noticed that many young people value their digital life as much (if not more) than their real life.[2]

While the Internet is growing, our real friendships are shrinking.

The Knight-Ridder news service recently released a study indicating that Americans are reporting fewer and fewer close friends.[3] In 1985, pollsters noted that the average person reported having three close friends; but by 2006, it was only two. And the number who say they have no one to discuss important matters with has doubled to one in four.[4] The social implications are significant—from no friends to visit you in the hospital, and weakened friendship bonds during crisis, to fewer watchdogs to deter neighborhood crime, and a lack of community.

From a church and ministry perspective, this trend has significant implications. As Shane Hipps relates in his book *The Hidden Power of Electronic Culture*:

Churches have begun to use blogs, chat areas, and electronic bulletin boards in their efforts to build community. Yet there remains the danger of people finding connection through these electronic forms and believing they have found genuine intimacy. This can cause them to miss out on authentic community with the people they worship with each week.[5]

As I write this, *USA Today* published a story called "Meet my 5,000 new best pals." It's about the phenomenal growth of online "friends" that use social media for community. Although the teenager featured in the story lists 5,036 friends on her site, she admits that she has virtually no relationship with at least 90 percent of those people. Today, "friending," as they call it, has become a status symbol, with many young people afraid to start college without hundreds of online "friends" to give them some sort of perceived validity.[6]

Friendships without relationship—it's new territory for most of us.

I was struck a few years ago when my assistant traveled to South Carolina to attend her grandmother's funeral. Even though I grew up in nearby North Carolina, it was a welcome reminder of the sense of community a small town engenders. After the funeral service itself, my assistant was astonished at the number of church members, former co-workers and friends who came to the family home with fried chicken, casseroles, vegetables, cake, pies and other food for the family. They turned out in huge numbers to simply sit with the family and comfort them.

> When you die, how many of your Facebook friends will come to comfort your family? How many Internet chat room members will show up at the funeral?

Addicted to Electronic Connection

I used to enjoy the radio or CD player when driving, but now I feel compelled to do business on my mobile device. I can't seem to sit in a car by myself without "doing something." At the same time, I've become a Zen master at email. I can download it through wired or wireless connections, my cell card or from any other computer on the planet. But I try to control that impulse now.

While filming a project in London, I had an experience that shocked me into realizing how much I needed boundaries around my email habits. Kathleen and I had finished breakfast and were waiting in the lobby for the film crew to bring our vehicles around to the front of the hotel. While waiting, I decided to visit the restroom, where I encountered a professional-looking businessman.

I noticed that at the same time he was using the restroom, he was also checking his email on his mobile device. I couldn't help myself, so I leaned over and said, "Brother, that's bondage."

He replied in a perfect British accent, "Sir, you have no idea how serious this bondage is."

I walked out of that restroom, pulled my iPhone out of my pocket and gave it to Kathleen. I decided right then that I never want to get to the place where I feel such a compulsion to answer my email.

I believe I am not mistaken when I say that Christianity is a demanding and serious religion. When it is delivered as easy and amusing, it is another kind of religion altogether.

Neil Postman
Media Critic

The Trivial Culture

Another great concern about a media-driven culture is television's tendency to trivialize everything it touches. In an earlier age, pastors and ministry leaders were brilliant thinkers and intellectuals. Men like Jonathan Edwards, George Whitefield and Charles Finney were all highly educated and had exceptional speaking and writing skills. It was typical of their time to speak for more than two hours; and during public debates, each side would speak for at least an hour, back and forth, so that the entire event unfolded over a five-to six-hour period.

I grew up in the South attending evangelistic "camp meetings" with my grandmother. Many of these meetings were virtual festivals, with picnics, activities for the kids, potluck dinners on the grounds and even overnight housing; and very often, the preaching would last all day and far into the evening. One of my earliest memories is of sitting on a handmade quilt on a sawdust floor, listening to preachers pound the pulpit long past my bedtime.

Compare that time frame to the length of programming for typical television preachers today. With most programs running 30 minutes, by the time we edit the opening, closing, a couple of special video segments or product offers and perhaps an interview, the preaching segment gets little more than 12 to 16 minutes on most programs. That time constraint has also trickled down into many Sunday services as well. I visited a church, just a few weeks ago, in which the pastor preaches no more than 12 to 15 minutes on a Sunday. He feels that in a highly distracted culture, 15 minutes is about all he can demand of his audience.

> ### Sadly, it's not about raising the congregation to a higher level; it's about bringing the ministry down to theirs.

Much of what we call worship has become show business, as pastors feel the need to entertain congregations in order to justify their time. As a media producer (and an easily distracted person myself), I'm the first to protest a boring service or anything that doesn't keep the momentum moving forward. I'm told that a journalist once asked suspense movie director Alfred Hitchcock about the perfect length for a movie. His reply was, "The length of a film should be directly related to the endurance of the human bladder."

I tend to feel the same way about church services.

At the same time, I wonder how the compulsion to entertain has damaged the sacred experience. After all, there is something to the mystery of our faith, and when Christianity is adapted to an entertainment medium, how much of the serious pursuit of the divine has been sacrificed? It's difficult to portray the transcendent through the same medium that broadcasts the World Wrestling Federation or *American Idol*. The result is the frustrating sight of our faith fraying around the edges.

One pastor dresses like Elvis every Sunday to draw more interest. Many churches mix movie clips with sermons, rock 'n' roll with worship, and sports metaphors with the services, all of which I often support.

Creativity is important, but at what expense?

In our well-intentioned efforts to reach the largest audience possible, we've forgotten that the Christian faith isn't always easy, and this generation is starting to recognize the disconnect.

One 30-year-old national magazine editor sent me an email recently that summed up the entire point. We'd been discussing the question of what's wrong with Christian television, and his response was a wake-up call: "Who cares? Anyone my age, who's grown up on television, knows you can't take anything you see on it seriously, whether it's religion or not. It's all trivial and ultimately doesn't matter. Television is an entertainment medium, so why would I ever watch a Christian program on TV?"

> Television has trivialized news, educational programming and politics.
> And now it has done the same to religion.

In his book *Amusing Ourselves to Death*, media critic and theorist Neil Postman describes the competing visions of the future of technology outlined by George Orwell in his book *1984*, and by Aldous Huxley in *Brave New World*:

What Orwell feared were those who would ban books. What Huxley feared was that there would be no reason to ban a book, for there would be no one who wanted to read one. Orwell feared those who would deprive us of information. Huxley feared those who would give us so much that we would be reduced to passivity and egoism. Orwell feared the truth would be concealed from us. Huxley feared the truth would be drowned in a sea of irrelevance. Orwell feared that we would become a captive culture. Huxley feared that we would become a trivial culture, preoccupied with some equivalent of the feelies, the orgy porgy, and the centrifugal bumblepuppy. As Huxley remarked in *Brave New World Revisited*, the civil libertarians and rationalists who are ever on the alert to oppose tyranny "failed to take into account man's almost infinite appetite for distractions." In short, Orwell feared that what we hate will ruin us. Huxley feared that what we love will ruin us.[7]

There is no question, Huxley was the prophetic voice. Thanks to television, we're consumed by the trivial. Thanks to the Internet, we are drowning in a sea of information and yet unable to truly communicate. And thanks to email, we live our lives under the compulsion that there's an important message out there that is worth interrupting everything else to read.

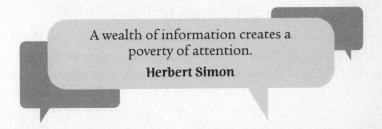

A wealth of information creates a poverty of attention.

Herbert Simon

In a digital age, authenticity may be the ultimate scorecard for success. But it's not the traditional definition of authenticity we're talking about here. In the past, authenticity had to do with *proof*.

A famous painting was authentic because it could be proven beyond a shadow of a doubt that it was real. A prized autograph was authentic because there was documentation to back up the claim. Authenticity used to be about truth; today it's about preference.

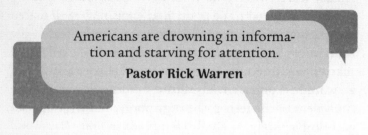

Americans are drowning in information and starving for attention.
Pastor Rick Warren

Today, authenticity has to do with *feeling*. When someone likes you or your ministry, they feel like you're "authentic." It has nothing to do with a qualitative decision, research or what is true; it's simply an emotional response. Be very careful when people describe you or your ministry as authentic, because in a postmodern value system, it's only meaning is that you resonate with that particular person.

It may be your clothing, mannerisms, age, personal style or type of program; but whatever it is, it probably has little to do with your ministry's real value or credibility. However, we still need to recognize the issue and respond.

Breaking the Spell of Trivialization

So how do we break the spell of trivialization? Do we take the Luddite path to oblivion or make a real attempt to wrestle the monster to the ground? I honestly don't hold much hope that the majority of Christian media will get much better. As a result, I believe there are two key strategies we must begin as soon as possible.

Key Strategy #1: Find Innovative Christian Communicators
First, we must find the innovative Christian communicators who really want to make a difference. While there will always be a place

in the media for important and timely preaching, that source of programming will not be the driver of Christian media as it has been in the past. Today there are independent producers creating low-budget movies, short films, Internet radio programming, innovative websites, podcasts, social media campaigns and more, and we must find them and encourage what they're doing.

The first generation of religious media communicators were, for the most part, pastors and evangelists who seized upon radio and eventually television as a way to extend their ministries. Their strength was the power of the message. They preached with passion and excitement and were relentless in their mission to spread the gospel.

Their weakness was packaging—the various elements such as lighting, set design, wardrobe, directing and editing that make up a quality program. They were preachers, after all, and had little idea of creativity, production techniques, contemporary graphics, branding or compelling visuals. Their resulting programs shared an important message but were often corny, low quality and poorly produced. To nonbelievers, they appeared fake, cheesy and insincere.

Today the driving force behind Christian media is emerging from behind the camera. Young creatives want to expand the horizon of religious media, try new techniques and create projects for wide-ranging audiences. These producers are looking beyond telethons to fund their projects and are experimenting with commercial sponsorship, grants, product placement, and more.

And now, preachers are catching the vision as well. Just because you preach doesn't mean the program has to be old-fashioned; and through innovative production techniques, a younger generation of pastors and ministry leaders are discovering how to reach an audience and create a response.

Key Strategy #2: Expand the Conversation

Second, we need to continue this conversation and expand it through our personal networks. Once we understand the trivializing nature of television, for instance, it loses its power over us. If we can teach men, women and families how to consume media correctly, we can make huge strides in using it more effectively. I always encourage pastors to have "movie nights" at church to view current films and engage the audience in a discussion. The media is the single greatest influence over the members of your congregation, and yet few pastors teach about its impact and effects.

We've allowed an entire generation to grow up helpless in the face of a force that literally consumes their lives. Teach about it, discuss it and keep this conversation going. As innovative writer and pastor Erwin McManus said a few years ago to an audience at the National Religious Broadcasters conference:

> God is already having a conversation with the culture, and our job is to intersect that conversation where *they* are, not where *we* are. We've got to move away from creating programming that is comfortable for us, into programming that engages the audience where they are at the moment.[8]

Never have Christians pursued relevance more strenuously; never have Christians been more irrelevant.

Os Guinness

The Danger of Chasing Relevance

Ask a typical pastor or ministry leader what they want to accomplish with their ministry, programs or products, and chances are that you'll hear the words "be relevant." "Relevance" has become the hot buzzword today—especially in the Christian media world—and applies to church services, TV and radio programming, books, music and outreaches of all kinds. In this culture, everyone wants to be relevant.

I've spent my career helping the Church speak the language of the culture; and being contemporary and relevant is part of that equation. In that process, I've discovered that most people work so hard to be relevant that they spin hopelessly into irrelevance.

How? Most pastors and Christian leaders mistake relevant for trendy. They hope that if they wear the right clothes, use the right words, get just the right haircut, speak on current topics or play the right music, they'll somehow be perceived as relevant.

The Bible doesn't need you to make it relevant. It's already relevant.

Robyn Waters has written the insightful book *The Trendmaster's Guide: Get a Jump on What Your Customer Wants Next*. It has become a popular guide for business and marketing directors trying to create the next hot product based on current trends. I bought the book expecting to find out just how silly and shallow American business has become; but as I read, I realized that the writer was onto something that most pastors and Christian leaders have missed about tracking trends:

> Trends are indicators that point to what's going on in the hearts and minds of consumers. And there's a big difference between a trend tracker and a Trendmaster. A trend tracker looks at the signs to help his or her business stay up to the minute. A Trendmaster, however, uses the trend information to determine where that minute is going. Trendmasters start out by observing a trend, but then they translate that trend information into a direction that makes sense for their companies and their customers.[9]

Jesus was upset at the religious leaders of His day because they knew how to interpret the appearance of the sky, but they didn't understand the signs of the times. It's not about chasing the latest new thing; it's about interpreting what that new thing means to your audience.

> ## Being relevant is something far bigger and more significant that constantly trying to figure out what's next.

Robyn Waters goes on to say, "It's easy to get caught up in the frenzy of tracking trends and to forget about the really good things that seem to last forever. Don't be so focused on the next big thing that you forget about those things that are always in style."[10]

> ## Relevance isn't about chasing trends; it's about standing the test of time.

The French philosopher and culture critic Simone Weil said, "To be always relevant, you have to say things which are eternal." Ultimate relevance is about the principles that last—eternal Truths with a capital *T*.

That's no excuse to wear tasteless clothes, sport bad haircuts, have a choir with no talent, or use out-of-date techniques. (I'd like to start a museum of bad Christian TV, but I can't find a building big enough.) To speak in the living room of the society, you must first get in the door. In Acts 17, the apostle Paul gave us the perfect example of how to engage the culture, and it still resonates today, especially when it comes to the media: No matter how brilliant your message, it doesn't matter if no one listens.

When they do listen, make sure you're not trying to chase relevance. In that vain search, we've exchanged powerful preaching for positive thinking; we've exchanged classic Christian doctrines for "what's practical"; and we've exchanged our unique calling to become simply another lifestyle choice.

Without a clear vision of our unique character and purpose before the world, we've uncritically adopted business principles, marketing savvy and pop culture. Os Guinness wrote, "A great part of the evangelical community has made an historic shift. It has transferred authority from *Sola Scriptura* (by Scripture alone) to *Sola Cultura* (by culture alone)."[11]

> From the legacy of a world in which
> Martin Luther stood up to the secular powers
> and said, "Here I stand, so help me God, I can do no
> other"; or William Tyndale, who defied the
> British crown and was strangled and burned
> at the stake for giving us the remarkable gift of the Bible
> in English, today we have turned from God's authority
> to the authority of the culture.

In our well-intentioned efforts to draw large audiences, expand our congregations and increase our impact in the world, we've lost our unique character before the world to the point where the culture sees little difference between becoming a Christian and becoming a Lakers fan.

As Philip D. Kenneson and James L. Street wrote in their book *Selling Out the Church*, "The marketing mentality readily assumes that the church of Jesus Christ is fundamentally like other organizations and businesses."[12]

Chasing relevance is a hopeless proposition, because what's relevant changes as styles, trends and seasons change. What was wonderfully relevant last year might simply get a laugh now.

Instead, we must build our lives and ministries around the eternal verities—the things that last, that are eternal.

It doesn't matter if you're a pastor, ministry leader, filmmaker, artist or business leader. If you want to be remembered and have your message mean as much to someone 100 years from now as it does at this moment, then reach for a higher goal.

Ultimately, to truly be relevant, you have to stop trying so hard to be relevant.

The Marketing Conflict

From my earliest exposure to marketing in graduate school, I discovered that *marketing* is far more than just advertising and selling a product; it's a very complex discipline involving pricing formulas, financial markets, packaging research, strategy, demographics and the business/customer exchange.

> Church marketers overlook that Jesus, in being faithful to his calling, also drove people away. Some of Jesus' most radical and disturbing teachings were given at junctures when crowds were the largest.
>
> **Philip Kenneson and James Street**
> *Selling Out the Church*[13]

In fact, in 1985, the American Marketing Association articulated it this way:

Marketing is the process of planning and executing the conception, pricing, promotion, and distribution of ideas, goods and services to create exchanges that will satisfy individual and organizational objectives.[14]

I focus on this issue because in the vast majority of religious organizations (as in the vast majority of companies), few people really understand the concept of marketing. I've sat in meetings where someone was assigned the position of marketing director simply because that person had experience in sales. Or a graphic designer became marketing director because people assumed she understood advertising. Or in the worst cases, the company president or business leader has a son or daughter who seems to be "creative," so they get assigned to the marketing department.

Most church and ministry marketing
efforts are not only inept, but they're also catastrophic.
In fact, I would put forth that marketing
may be one of the most misused techniques
and disciplines in the church today.

Is marketing important?
Absolutely.
Then why do we screw it up?
I would suggest a new definition of marketing when it comes
to the work of the church:

When I view my role as a branding or
media consultant, I view that role as simply placing
the church or ministry in the best possible light.

It's that simple.
My job is to put as many people as possible in front of that
pastor, evangelist, radio or television program, movie, website, social media campaign or event. Then, I expect that pastor to preach
a message without compromise and with the power that comes
from the anointing of the Holy Spirit. My goal is for people to have
a life-changing encounter with God. But if the message drives
them away—as Jesus' often did—that's their choice.

For too many years, the church has tried to pre-qualify its audience. We only wanted people who were cleaned up and well man-
nered. We wanted people who dressed up for services. We wanted
people of a certain income or race. Worse, we tried lame promotional gimmicks to generate a crowd.

These were well-meaning people who had the the best of intentions. I've discovered that when it comes to marketing a
church, even the worst offenders are motivated by the right purpose: the goal of reaching out to the largest audience possible. As
a result, while I like to enjoy poking fun at some of the Christian
stunts and "Jesus Junk" out there (jesusjunk.com), I'm not a cynic.

I don't take the path of those who ridicule, humiliate or criticize people as if they were purposely trying to damage the character and reputation of the Church (although that's exactly what sometimes happens).

In 2006, a respected Australian broadcaster named Andrew Denton produced a documentary film on the National Religious Broadcasters. Originally, his intention was to document how faith informed President George Bush's politics; but on a stop at the national convention of Christian broadcasters, he was mesmerized. He interviewed numerous personalities in the industry (including me) over the five-day period the convention took place. But the most interesting scenes were filmed simply walking up and down the aisles of the exhibit halls at the event as he talked to people at random.

He interviewed people selling TV time, marketing new and unique Bibles, bronze sculptures, health food, religious trinkets, trips to Israel, and much more. Many of the booths had nothing overtly to do with broadcasting, but they were more than eager to be interviewed on television.

There were a lot of odd folks in the mix, and Andrew brilliantly just let them talk. He didn't condemn or embarrass; he simply let them tell their story, and by doing so, they often made themselves look strange and out of touch with the culture.

It was a perfect example of some people who have been communicating the same way for decades; while the culture has changed, they've held the course. Now they seem outdated, out of touch and quaint. They are the leftovers of the early days of the industry, the ones who are supposed to be professional Christian communicators but have little connection to a mainstream audience today.

By the time Andrew interviewed me, he was fascinated with religious broadcasters, and we had a lively discussion of the strengths and weaknesses of using the media to impact the culture with a religious message.

The resulting film was called *God on My Side* and debuted at a highly regarded film festival in Sydney, Australia, followed up by a theatrical movie release across the country, and eventually a prime-time broadcast on a major Australian TV network.

I was speaking at a media conference in Australia a year or so later, and my wife and I sat down with Andrew at a coffee shop across the street from his office to discuss the movie and to catch up. He said that after the broadcast of his documentary, he was disconcerted at some friends who told him, "Good job, Andrew. Way to stick it to those con-artists in religious media." Others were thrilled that he had somehow exposed the charlatans in the Christian broadcasting world.

Andrew told them they had missed the point. He said that the one thing he walked away with from the religious broadcasting conference was that, above all, these were absolutely sincere people. They honestly believed in what they were doing and were committed to what they believed was right—so much so that it was actually surprising, and moving to him as well.

And yet, the overall response to the film was how inept, crooked and out of touch Christian broadcasters seem to the world. The vast majority of the film was simply letting the people talk and tell their stories.

Much of the Church is plagued by well-meaning individuals who damage our credibility and witness because they express their faith in a way that seems so insincere, out of touch and odd.

Good People, Bad Ideas

What we need to realize is the fundamental point of being *in* the world but not *of* the world. This is a very real tension between wanting to attract the largest possible audience while knowing that our very message will drive many away.

When I work with secular companies, our marketing goal is to remove anything that would hinder the full acceptance of the product. We want potential customers to fall in love with our athletic shoes, coffee, furniture or candy. We want to fix anything that could possibly be a reason they might hesitate to purchase the product.

But with the Christian faith, our goal is a bit different. We want as many people as possible to have the opportunity to hear the gospel, but we also know that we can't compromise, water down or modify the product. Maintaining the integrity of the Christian message is without discussion or debate. Therefore, we aim high, knowing that some seed will fall on rocky places.

Not everyone will get through the narrow way (see Matt. 7:14).

In Acts 2, it is recorded that about 3,000 people were added to the Church in one day. That's a marketer's dream. After all, living things grow. The Church should be growing and its outreaches expanding. I believe very strongly in the marketing principles of getting the message out, sharing it in the best possible way and then believing God for the harvest.

That last element—believing God for the harvest—might be another very misunderstood element of church and ministry marketing. I can't guarantee success to my clients. In fact, it's not my job. God gives the increase. We can plan, create brilliant advertising materials, promote the event in the best possible light and attract thousands. But once the message is preached or shared, the convicting power of the Holy Spirit takes over. In that sense, it's not my job to win the lost; it's God's.

Many people rightly criticize church and ministry marketing because they've seen it done so poorly, they have inaccurate expectations of the results or they rightly worry about its excesses. I've discovered that the two key things to consider in effective marketing should be: First, don't change who you are; second, stop trying to make the church identical to every other organization in the culture.

Don't Change Who You Are
You are who you are. God has called you to be unique and different. The world isn't looking for another Mark Driscoll, John Piper, Joel Osteen, Joyce Meyer, Steven Furtick, Billy Graham, Tony Evans, Matthew Barnett, or T. D. Jakes. They just might be looking for *you*. If an advertising or marketing consultant tries to change your

change your unique style, gifts or calling, then you're on the wrong track from the beginning. A great marketer will take the time to understand who you are, what your personal and ministry gifts are, what your vision for ministry really is, and then focus on that. It's not about *changing* your calling; it's about *celebrating* your calling.

Should you change that dumpy suit, a bad accent or the purple carpet in the church? Probably. Don't let a bad package prequalify your audience. Remove any boundaries that would keep people from hearing your message; but in the process, don't lose the message itself.

Stop Trying to Make Your Church Like All the Others

In our well-intentioned effort to make the secular culture comfortable with the Christian message, we often take away the very things that make us distinctive. People don't worry that screaming fans will turn off potential ticket buyers for football games, that traditional customs at Jewish weddings will drive friends away, or that weird initiation rites will stop college students from joining fraternities and sororities.

And yet, today we're terrified that raising our hands in church will hurt attendance, that prayer for the sick will make us seem cultic, or that baptism during the Sunday service would seem out of place.

At a national media conference sponsored by a major religious denomination, I had the opportunity to meet with the head of communication for the entire organization. I asked him about the biggest challenge the denomination was facing.

He replied, "Oh, that's simple. It's drums."

"Drums?"

"That's right. We may even have a national schism over the use of drums in the church. It's a huge battle right now, and it's literally tearing some churches apart."

I sat there in shock for a minute, and then said, "I thought that was a bridge we crossed in the sixties and seventies in most churches."

"Not in ours," he said.

We major in the minors while the real distinctiveness of our faith is lost to the world.

Certainly negative issues like doctrinal errors, a poorly prepared sermon or a church with no vision should be examined, but in the process, we can't lose the positive distinctives that have made the Christian Church a force that transformed Western civilization.

Phil Pringle pastors Christian City Church in Oxford Falls, Australia, a suburb of Sydney. A few years ago, I visited the church and spent some time talking with him about his love of the media and how it has impacted the church. Phil has been frustrated by the limitations of traditional Christian radio and television, so he's exploring social media and he posts short videos online on a regular basis. I asked him about his branding, and he said something very interesting. His family comes from the Pentecostal tradition, and early in his ministry he saw many other growing churches pulling away from their Pentecostal and charismatic roots. In an effort to reach the widest possible audience, they were changing their worship and preaching style to something more middle of the road.

Seeing that change happening to so many churches, Phil did just the opposite. He realized that his distinctive was his Pentecostal tradition; so rather than back away like so many others were doing, he focused on the gifts of the Spirit. As a result, his church has exploded, and a new generation of young people looking for a profound charismatic and Pentecostal experience is flocking to the church.

Phil Pringle understands the power of being distinctive in ministry.

> ### Effective marketing doesn't mean making the church appear like a stockholders' meeting at IBM.

Perhaps we've had to rely on marketing simply because nothing else is happening inside the church itself. The great tragedy today is how anemic so many churches have become. Three thousand people were added to the Early Church in one day because Peter preached a message of power and authority. The Bible reports that the audience was "cut to the heart" and immediately asked, "What shall we do?" (see Acts 2:37).

Now that's action! That's direct response. That's results.

According to recent research, most Christians in this country live virtually identical lives to non-Christians. We watch the same TV programs and movies, experience divorce at about the same rate as the secular culture, and have become accommodating to a fault. As a result, we've lost any real reason for the world to become attracted to or intrigued with us.

In this sense, marketing has been forced to plug a hole that supernatural power and authority used to fill.

Compromising Our Identity

In the book *Biblical Perspectives on Evangelism: Living in a Three-Storied Universe*, theologian Walter Brueggemann comments on the Old Testament nation of Israel's accommodation:

> In the disciplines of fasting and sackcloth, the Israelites "separated themselves from all foreigners" and confessed their sin (Nehemiah 9:1-2). This act in the drama needs to be understood carefully. Wrongly understood, according to Christian stereotypes of Jews, this separation sounds like arrogant legalism. Such a view misses the point completely. Rather, this community in its amnesia had assimilated itself, domesticated its memory, and compromised its identity, so that it had nothing left of itself. Judaism had become such a detrimental embarrassment, that Jews had worked to overcome their Jewishness. And now, in these dangerous liturgical acts, Jews are facing up to their oddity, to their strong commitment, to their distinctive obedience. The recovery of

distinctiveness entails the acceptance of an odd identity. I report this point to you because I believe the church in the United States faces a crisis of accommodation and compromise that is near to final evaporation. Note well, the distinctiveness is not in doctrine or in morality, but in memory. For the text adds that all through this time of separation, "They stood up in their place and read from the book of the law.[15]

Remember the *Unique Selling Proposition*—what makes a product different from every other product in the marketplace. What makes the Church different and unique today?

Hopefully, it's more than the snappy design of your church newsletter.

Understand and Deal with the Tension of the Marketing Conflict

The Christian life is hard, there's no doubt about it. People who gave up everything to follow Christ have been burned at the stake, crucified upside down, boiled alive, dismembered, imprisoned and disgraced. Today, we live in the most democratic and free society in the history of the Church, but that freedom has lulled us into cultural accommodation. As a result, we've lost our focus on the hard sayings of Jesus and tried to refocus on what God supposedly says about buying a Mercedes, owning a private jet or having a coffee bar at church.

Don't get me wrong. None of these things are inherently evil or immoral. (I stand for hours in security lines at airports dreaming about owning a private jet.) But I worry that we've so strongly bought into the American way of life that we've become more identified with capitalism and democracy than with faith. As we've grown in political power, we're becoming known as the people who are *against* everything instead of the people who are *for* something.

Have we lost our moral authority in the culture by trading it in for a larger network TV audience?

Is there an answer? If you look deeply into the issue, I really don't think so, which is exactly why the marketing conflict exists. We can plead a life of poverty until we realize that reaching a mass audience through the media costs millions of dollars. We can make a hard stand for an issue until we realize that without some negotiation we'll never have much influence in society. We can be strident about public morality until we come up against other belief systems that want an equal voice in the conversation. As Brueggemann points out, the Jewish nation wrestled with the divisive issue of cultural accommodation thousands of years ago, so this is nothing new.

That doesn't cause us to stop, but it does make us aware of the tension involved in presenting our message to a twenty-first-century audience.

Financial challenges are a great example. Pastor Gary Keesee in Columbus, Ohio, was a financial planner before he was called into ministry. From that unique perspective, he likes to say, "You'll never achieve your destiny until you get the money thing fixed." For instance, just try to walk away from your job and be a missionary with a huge financial debt hanging over your head, or attempt to go into full-time ministry with a poor record of balancing a budget. Without a miracle, you're in for a real challenge.

Life happens. As fallen creatures, we live in conflict every day.

But many refuse to accept the conflict. On the one hand, some Christian marketing "experts" relentlessly extol the virtues of marketing churches and ministries with little regard for the damage it can cause. On the other hand, academics and ministry leaders have written carloads of books decrying marketing as the end of the church as we know it.

Meanwhile, somewhere in the middle, we wrestle with the task of getting the Christian message to as many people as possible, and at the same time, keeping the church distinctive and unique without making us look weird and crazy.

The conflict will always be there. Our goal is to seek balance. We want to get people into the seats without harming the integrity or perception of the church as a life-changing entity, and yet extend grace to those who walk away in spite of our best efforts.

Academics or critics can sit at a distance and make their pronouncements, but for those of us in the trenches, wrestling with that conflict is a way of life.

Take Your **Thinking Deeper**

1. Do you give much thought to the *purpose* and *place* of technology, or do you just accept it without question? Is there a time to take a *media fast* and reestablish relationships directly with people?

2. What are you doing to help your children navigate today's media culture? Are you training them with the expertise and tools to make mature decisions?

3. Do you *intentionally* carve out time for deeper thinking, book reading, serious movies, discussions, devotional time, and more? Or are you living under the tyranny of clichés we see with most TV, popular magazines and social media?

4. Who are the communicators you see out there who are sharing a significant message that really matters today?

5. How much time at your organization or in your work do you spend chasing trends rather than pursuing what really matters?

6. Do you take time on a regular basis to do a "communications audit" of your organization? Ask yourself: Is

our marketing strategy making a difference? Are we really communicating the right message? Is our communications and media strategy a force for good in the world?

7. Remember that branding isn't becoming someone else; it's discovering who you really are. Take time periodically to think about that. Are your communications and marketing efforts telling the *real* story? Are you really being authentic in your advertising and the other ways you share the message?

The Branding Imperative

> A generation ago the question was, "What is truth?" Today, the question is, "What's the point?"
>
> **Billy Graham**

Branding is not foolproof, and it's not a magic bullet. In the secular world, the most brilliant advertising campaign can't make a bad product a success; and in the religious world, branding can't cover up serious ministry mistakes or hypocrisy. Moral failure, bad management or spiritual apathy cannot be "fixed" by a great brand. Integrity matters.

Real branding is about creating and maintaining trust; without delivery on that trust, the relationship is broken. A number of years ago, I was asked to create a new brand for a national ministry client. It was a perfect situation. The ministry leader was articulate, driven to excellence and committed, and he had a powerful message to share. As a result, we created a new look and feel for the ministry, designed a powerful identity and were able to unify that look and feel throughout the ministry's television outreach, website, print materials, social media presence, and more.

But we quickly discovered a problem: customer service. The client organization had a corrupt computer database of supporters, so I immediately brought in an expert at analyzing and evaluating those types of data-related problems. Usually, it was not a big deal; but the first challenge we encountered was a ministry team that cared little about customer service. As a result, they refused to acknowledge the corrupted data; in a futile attempt to save face, they spent months denying it was an issue. Because we refused to let go, they finally were forced to admit there was a problem, and it was significant indeed.

People would purchase products from the ministry and wait months to receive them. They would make donations without receiving a thank-you or further follow-up. First-time donors were dropped out of the system without being encouraged to become regular givers. Worse, John Q. Public from Tulsa was getting John Q. Public from Cleveland's product orders, and vice versa.

It was a nightmare.

It took more than a year to resolve the crisis, partly because of the level of corruption in the file, and partly because of the obstinacy of the staff. They refused to act on the problem for fear of looking inept, and then they refused to believe it was serious until it was too late.

At that one ministry alone, I calculated that they lost millions of dollars in potential donations from supporters who felt angry and frustrated and eventually left because of the way they were treated. One of my great frustrations with the client was how our branding changes were generating far more responses through television and the Web, but those new people would soon become so frustrated they would walk away. It's hard enough to get the phones to ring in the first place, but then allowing them to slip through your fingers is inexcusable.

You cannot put a price tag on great customer service. Don't let your calling, gifts and talents get damaged because of uncaring or unprofessional staff members. Customer service is vital in a secular business, but it's absolutely critical in religious and non-profit work. Acquiring a new customer is five times more expensive than keeping a current customer happy. Finding new customers is more thrilling, and keeping old customers is hard work. But the truth is, you'll profit far more by keeping people than by having to constantly find new ones.

We call the places where a customer or potential supporter encounters your organization a "touch point," and it's vital that they receive the best treatment possible, no matter where they choose to encounter the ministry. Telephone operators, mailing and shipping staff, tour guides, media directors, ushers, Sunday School teachers and workers, marketing people—anyone who could possibly meet a customer, church member or supporter needs to understand just how important they are and who they represent.

> It doesn't matter how much you spend on marketing your church, how much you prepare your message or how anointed you are in the pulpit. If a new visitor walks in and meets a grumpy usher, that's your brand in his or her mind.

Employee Evangelists

A few years ago, I was unexpectedly caught at an airport when a major snowstorm blew in. Hundreds of flights were cancelled, stranding thousands of frustrated people on the ground. The airline I was flying was a major company with thousands of employees. They had spent millions developing their brand, millions more on advertising and public relations, and had hired some of the top executives in the airline industry. But that night, for thousands of their customers, that airline wasn't represented by its CEO, its top executives or its advertising gurus; it was represented by the men and women at the ticket counter—the people on the front line.

Had they dropped the ball, no amount of advertising and branding could have fixed the perception in the mind of their customers.

Remember, your employees are the embodiment of your brand. Your brand story has to trickle down to everyone in your organization. Make every employee an evangelist for your story. Just as a salesman at a department store represents that store to a customer, the ministry employees that your audience, visitors, supporters or congregation come in contact with are your brand.

When it comes to customer service, branding consultant Wally Olins has a list of simple rules for keeping your service up to par.

1. *Organize your operation around the brand.* In other words, get everyone in your organization talking to each other. Do you remember when you started and your team consisted of three or four people? Everyone was on the same page simply because you were probably all in the same room. But we grow and people stop talking to each other. Little kingdoms get set up around the church and ministry, and before long, people start fighting over budgets, status and who knows what else.

   In an effort to get everyone on the same page, I have some clients who have done away with titles to get rid of the inside politics and competition. Other clients provide everyone the same size office and furniture. In what I would consider an act of desperation, one major church has their leadership staff switch jobs every year or so to keep them guessing (which also keeps them, in my opinion, terrified).

   Certainly there are problems with each of these techniques, but I understand the motivation. The important thing to remember is that it's a Herculean effort to keep everyone working together without pride, or ego, rearing its ugly head. Whatever your strategy, keep people talking and focus that discussion on the brand.

2. *Train your people to live the brand.* If they don't buy into the vision, they are working against it. That's why so many companies have off-site retreats, team-building activities, training classes, and more.

3. *Behave the way you talk.* Do your people model the behavior they are supposed to be representing? Do they represent the organization well? It's one thing to be caught in a strip club when you work for a cell phone company. It's another thing altogether to be caught in a strip club while working for a church.

4. *Always remember that your staff is the brand.* A surly salesperson can forever sour you on the entire company, and an unfriendly usher can do the same.

5. *Be consistent and coherent.* Make sure the customer experience is uniform throughout the organization.

6. *Treat customers with respect.* Don't let your people get complacent. Your supporters are your lifeline and should never be taken for granted.

7. *Listen to customers' complaints.* Through personal outbound phone calls, mail or Web surveys and other techniques, listen to people. Find out how you're doing, and get regular feedback from the people who encounter your organization the most.

8. *Lead by example from the top.* It starts with the leader, and there is no substitute for someone who can cast the vision, set a spiritual and moral example, and make the tough decisions necessary to keep the vision alive.

9. *Trust your people to live the brand.* One of the greatest challenges to successful branding is the rigid organizational chart of many companies, churches and ministries. Once you reach a certain size, hardcore lines of demarcation are drawn and the walls go up. As a result, the sales staff doesn't talk to the designers;

accounting doesn't communicate with operations; and creative doesn't talk to the executives. Nation states get set up, kingdoms are created and the company becomes something completely inorganic and inflexible. In organizations where everyone wants to do it their way, getting a new brand identity to permeate those layers of management is nearly impossible.[1]

It's warfare for hearts and minds here. For a new brand to work, take extra pains to create unity and teamwork among your people. Ask them to share how the vision is played out in their respective departments and how the brand speaks to exactly how they contribute to the bottom line.

When I produce a television special or a film, I meet individually with each department head and ask how he or she plans to tell the story of the movie through his or her respective craft. For instance, what wardrobe choices will tell the story most effectively? What lighting decisions will help each scene tell the story? How will the makeup, editing, set design and all the other elements that make a movie tell the story from their individual perspectives?

When each employee understands how his department, craft or task fits into the brand story of your organization, you'll have a team that's firing on all cylinders and finally feels part of the process.

We must reject the idea—
well intentioned, but dead wrong—
that the primary path to greatness in
the social sectors is to become
"more like a business."

Jim Collins
Good to Great

When Business and Ministry Collide

The idea that a church, ministry or nonprofit must run like a business has gained enormous momentum in the last two decades. The world is exploding with business books by a variety of gurus and supposed experts. As a result, business thinking has become accepted dogma in religious organizations. I've always been an advocate of this development, because over the years, after working with more than 1,000 churches and ministries worldwide, I've discovered that religious organizations are often the worst-run operations on the planet.

Much of that difficulty comes from the tension between performance and loyalty. Naturally, in a religious organization, profit isn't the bottom line, and therefore, performance isn't as emphasized as much as it should be. As a result, churches and ministries are filled with wonderful but incompetent people. These employees and volunteers are committed to the organization, and they have integrity and are good people, but they've often been promoted through the years because of loyalty rather than expertise.

I know of one major church with a single employee I have estimated costs the organization at least $100,000 per year through sheer incompetence. She's responsible for the marketing efforts of the church, but she misses print and advertising deadlines, makes costly mistakes in product shipping, doesn't know how to evaluate advertising campaigns, and her decisions on any number of issues are usually wrong. She has no experience in marketing but was promoted to the position after being a loyal and capable assistant to the pastor for many years.

Employees of one church on the West Coast actually have a rather sick joke that to be fired, you'd have to show up at a shopping mall with a machine gun and shoot a few people. A job in that organization is pretty much a job for life, no matter how poorly you might perform any given position. The lack of competence, poor stewardship and resultant mismanagement of the congregation's money boggles the mind.

In another major ministry, poor management created an atmosphere of insecurity and terror throughout the organization. One incompetent senior ministry executive spent years managing employees through fear disguised as concern. For instance, when an employee would make a mistake, he would sit him or her down, express compassion and then tell the person, "I'm really worried that the pastor will find out about this. If that happens, he'll fire you for sure." Much like Absalom at the city gate, he would pretend to be concerned about people but, in reality, he was buying their loyalty and using fear to undermine the pastor.

Completely unknown to the pastor, this manager was terrorizing people and then pointing the finger at *him*. When I discovered the problem and shared my assessment with the pastor, he completely denied the possibility. He couldn't imagine that his employees were afraid of him, and he flatly refused to believe it. But I asked him to spend a few weeks "walking through the factory," casually spending time with employees, gaining their confidence and listening to them.

Sure enough, during my next visit a few months later, he pulled me aside and said that I was right. Employees of the ministry were terrified of him and thought he ruled with an iron hand. He eventually fired the senior executive, but it took years to completely repair the damage and change the perceptions of his employees.

Spend time with employees and volunteers— that means listening time, not just talking time.

Speaking of walking through the factory, let me share one of the most important secrets of managing a successful church or ministry: Spend time with employees and volunteers. Whenever we brand a ministry, it's critical to understand the thinking of your people; and the only way to do it is to listen. You'd probably be surprised at the number of corporate executives, church pastors and nonprofit leaders who rarely spend time with employees or volunteers. I know some that haven't visited sections of the building in years.

In some cases, ministry leaders spend little or no time with the media directors, graphic designers or writing staff—the very people who are the key to presenting that leader to a national media audience. They rarely hear him express his heart or have close contact, and then the leader wonders why he's not happy with the way he's being presented on national television or radio.

Don't automatically assume that everyone is on board with your vision or the direction of the new brand identity. It's critical that they feel you have their interests in mind, that you are listening and that you share their concerns.

Helping People Change

Having branded some of the major ministries in America, we're not oblivious to the fact that many employees or team members will either disagree with our approach or actively resist it. To a point, this is good. We certainly don't have all the answers; and a vibrant, relevant organization is one where disagreements happen, ideas are debated and directions are discussed.

But some organizations are paralyzed because they can't move from vibrant debate to unified action. To prepare you for potential disagreement, here are some of the key reasons why people resist change.

1. Love of Routine

Before he died, my father adored IHOP (the International House of Pancakes) and would eat there any time, any place. On the other side of the family, my father-in-law wouldn't think of touching a meal until he had a slice of bread with it. If the waiter brought the bread late, he would let his meal get cold before he would eat it.

Millions of people only fly on one airline, only drive a Chevy, get dressed in a certain order, can't function without that first cup of coffee. To do any of these things otherwise would drive them nuts.

I'm not a geneticist, so I don't know if it's our wiring or something we've acquired. All I know is that many people are slaves to routines that help them understand life, feel comfortable or make sense of things.

In many organizations, breaking work-related routines will chill some employees to the bone, so be ready for a fight. The key in these situations is to point out the *new* routine and how it will make their life better, generate more income, increase the bottom line, expand ministry, or whatever other benefit is true.

Years ago, I worked with a cameraman who couldn't function on location without a printed schedule. Whenever we changed the shooting plan or began to improvise, we would see him literally begin to sweat and get nervous. In those cases, I had our production manager create a fictional schedule. Although it meant absolutely nothing, he could hold it in his hand and feel like we had a direction and purpose for the day. The world was fine for him once again.

2. Potential Embarrassment and Survival

Change is often perceived as an unfair encroachment on a person's territory, and he or she worries about failing or looking bad—especially to superiors. This is understandable, but it's absolutely necessary that ministry employees comprehend that *change does not mean they've been doing something wrong*. This is not about mistakes; it's about responding to the changing culture with a fresh, new approach. We want everyone to embrace the change, take ownership of it and help us make it happen. A successful re-branding is something that happens from the inside.

That's why it's critically important to present the new branding effort in a positive light. It's not happening because we've screwed up; it's happening because we want to become more effective and move to the next level.

3. Miscommunication or Lack of Trust

What people don't understand, they will often resist. We must be clear about the change—why we're doing this, and how we're doing this. No one should feel left out; and we need to encourage everyone's ideas and suggestions. This is an exciting time for the ministry, and we need to enjoy the possibilities.

After my first meeting with one ministry, a key member of the media team abruptly quit his position. I didn't understand it, and on a future visit, I asked his wife, who worked in another department, about it. Her response was unexpected: "Well, Bob assumed that with the changes you want to make, he'll probably get fired anyway, so he decided the best thing to do was to go ahead and resign."

Amazing. I had no intention of firing him, but he was so misinformed and lacked trust in the ministry's ability to do the right thing that he purposely cut himself out of what became one of our most successful branding experiences.

4. Differing Ways of Evaluating Success

Because of their limited perspective, some employees may see the cost as greater than the benefits. There will always be people who are comfortable in their current situation, so the risk of change makes them extremely nervous. There certainly are financial costs related to change, but the cost in not changing can be catastrophic.

This is normally a case of limited vision for those outside the leadership team. While the leaders can see the big picture, we have to remember that employees in the media, missions, accounting, education or even the mailing and shipping departments may not have the same view. It's vital that we keep them informed and help them understand the scale we're using to evaluate success.

5. Poor Experiences with Previous Organizations

Sometimes I encounter an employee who went through a similar but badly executed experience in a previous organization. People were fired without cause; dramatic changes were thrust on employees without notice; or the creative strategy was flawed. As a result, they witnessed the disaster firsthand, and now they reflexively react in the negative when anything similar comes up.

The best solution here is taking the time to present the case for change and allowing employees to buy in to the process. Once they see the potential and understand the process of change, they begin to support the vision.

Always remember that when people think that something is their idea, they will fight to the death to make it happen. Don't dictate to your team; allow them to take ownership. President Ronald Reagan was right when he said the famous line, "There's no limit to what a man can accomplish, as long as it doesn't matter who gets the credit."

While working for one major media ministry, it didn't take me long to realize that the evangelist wanted people to think everything was his idea. So I would plant ideas in his head before the meetings. I would suggest alternate approaches, drop seeds of ideas in casual conversation, and make recommendations to him privately where no one else could hear.

Sure enough, usually on a three-day cycle, during production meetings, he would regurgitate my ideas as his own. But I discovered that when he thought the idea was his, he would do anything to make it work. It didn't bother me that he took the credit, because at least we were making good ideas happen.

6. Lack of Confidence in Management/Decision-Making Process
People don't believe that all the relevant information has been included in the process; something must be left out. Some leadership experts teach that an effective leader can and often should make a decision when he has at least 65 percent of the information he needs. Some executives put off changes, thinking, *If I just had one more piece of information* . . . Like rearranging deck chairs on the Titanic, we can keep discussing and waiting for more information while the organization slowly loses influence in the culture and eventually crashes around us.

Financial Results or Mission?

Change needs to happen in the church today; but because of the reasons people resist change, and other issues, reaching the point of positive change can be extraordinarily difficult. I spent years trying to translate solid business and leadership practices into church and nonprofit life. Certainly, in many cases, better management, organizational structure, discipline and techniques made a significant difference. There's no substitute for productivity, no matter what your goals, and much of the current business and leadership thinking can apply directly to challenges we face in the church and nonprofit world.

However, the more I worked with religious organizations and nonprofits, the more I realized there was a side effect as a result of the business principles I was teaching. In some cases, the techniques didn't get the same results they would have produced in a secular company; and in other cases, I was worried that we were turning pastors and nonprofit leaders into entrepreneurs who were more concerned about *bottom line* thinking than *mission* thinking.

Certainly, as I and others advocated better leadership, more disciplined organizational structure, accountability and more effective management techniques over the years, we began to see a much more professional attitude in many churches and ministries. Employee performance tightened up, finances were used more effectively, ministries became more effective, outreaches expanded and the perception about the organizations improved in the local community.

However, I also began to notice other, more disturbing, signs. I watched pastors transform themselves into corporate executives. I saw church and ministry managers become mobile device zombies, walking through the day with their eyes glued to their incoming email, and a corporate mentality that prioritized financial results over mission.

Recently, on a visit to a large church, I spent the day with the pastor, evaluating and advising on media ministry issues. But from the time the pastor picked me up at the hotel for breakfast until he dropped me off late that night after the evening service, he was held in bondage to his phone. Literally every 10 minutes he would glance at his email as if driven by some strange voodoo spell. During the day, we attended planning meetings with his top-level staff, attended a youth service and even looked in on a family during a counseling session. But no matter how intimate, serious or critical the moment, he continually allowed himself to be interrupted by the "ding" of an incoming email message.

I wanted to rip it out of his hand and scream at him that human contact was far more important than those little digital messages!

The executive mentality expresses itself in other ways as well:

- Pastors with schedules so busy they have little time for real human contact
- Hiring outside "professionals" for the kinds of church jobs that used to be driven by volunteers with a personal passion for ministry
- The substitution of software training for people skills
- A relentless drive for results instead of mission
- An overall attitude of structure that kills the loving attitude of fellowship (ushers forcing you to sit in certain places, high security systems, controlled access to certain areas of the church, the entourage of assistants [bodyguards?] that escort the pastor out of his car, into his office, onto the platform and back to his car again unmolested)

Certainly in a mega-church world, caution is in order. High-level security systems to protect children's areas are simply a necessary part of the culture now; and there's no question that with expensive computer, sound and lighting equipment, security is important. And it's impossible for each member of a church of 1,000 people or more to have all the private time he or she wants with the pastor.

But in the midst of these advances, I began to see "mission drift" in certain organizations when the focus went from community to commodity. When things and results generated the same concern and perceived value as people, I saw a distinct shift in the direction of pastors and ministry leaders.

Bookshelves in pastors' offices that had
previously been filled with volumes on theology,
Church history and doctrine have been replaced by the
latest bestsellers on business motivation and sales.

That's when I discovered a small monograph by Jim Collins, author of the business classic *Good to Great: Why Some Companies Make the Leap and Others Don't*. Apparently, Collins had been wrestling with many of the same issues in the nonprofit world, including groups like museums, youth programs and school outreaches, as well as churches. As a result, he wanted to adapt many of the "good to great" principles he'd discussed in his book; but this time, he focused on the social (or nonprofit and religious) sector of the economy.

Since the monograph was intended to be an addition to the book, he called it *Good to Great in the Social Sectors*. In it, he realized that businesses and nonprofit organizations were two different types of entities, and the same principles that drove one did not necessarily work for the other. He realized that the distinction wasn't about business or social:

> That's when it dawned on me: we need a new language.
> The critical distinction isn't between business and social,
> but between great and good. We need to reject the naïve
> imposition of the "language of business" on the social sectors, and instead, jointly embrace a language of greatness.[2]

Collins realized that trying to implement business principles in a church, ministry or other nonprofit organization does not work, because while business is driven by *financial returns*, a nonprofit is driven by *mission*. In other words, a business that doesn't make money is a loser, but nonprofits are "non-profit" by nature. Although we'd love it if we had all the money we needed, for most churches and ministries—even in an age of prosperity preaching— that's not what we're about, and it's not why we exist.

The Distinctives of Churches and Nonprofit Ministries

In the executive-driven world of many pastors, that critical distinction gets lost. But what does this mean for branding a typical church or ministry?

Driven by Meaning

Businesses are often driven by money, but nonprofit employees are driven by meaning. I'm certainly an advocate of paying people what they're worth when possible, but in most applications, nonprofits just can't compete with the salary scale of corporations. So instead of constantly worrying that you can't afford good employees, shift your search to people looking for meaning. They're out there, and they want to make a difference. If you have a strong vision and a compelling mission, chances are, there are people willing to work for a fraction of the money in order to be part of a greater project in life. Meaning is a powerful part of your brand, so keep the vision in front of the people, and keep it alive.

Results Quantified by the Mission

It's easy for a business to evaluate financial returns and product sales, but it's much more difficult for a church or ministry to quantify the results of mission. Working with gangs, feeding the homeless, evangelism, youth work, medical clinics, spiritual development, family counseling, teaching and training—these are much more difficult to apply to a chart-and-track progress, but it can be done.

In the old days, national ministries like those of Billy Graham, Oral Roberts and others kept detailed records of men and women converted at their meetings. They were very careful about recording that information and keeping it in front of their supporters and employees. I've personally read through thousands of the handwritten cards filled out by men and women at Oral Roberts's tent crusades back in the forties and fifties. Those men knew the value of quantifying their mission—not from an ego perspective but from the perspective of evaluating the results and staying on track.

Begin working with your leadership team to set benchmarks for mission. Fund-raising and product sales will always be important, but fund-raising results will always be more difficult without mission results.

Diversified Funding

With a business, income results from the sale of widgets. Certainly investment income, tax strategy, long-term planning and other policies play important roles, but the primary engine that drives corporate funding is sales. However, with a nonprofit, funding often comes from a wide variety of sources: individual tithing, large donors, grants, fellowships, partnership, product sales, capital campaigns, and more.

One of the constant challenges for nonprofits is funding, and the most successful ministry leaders are the men and women who understand the importance of casting a wide net. As Collins puts it, "The critical question is not 'How much money do we make?' but 'How can we develop a sustainable resource engine to deliver superior performance relative to our mission?'"

One of the issues most church leaders miss is the need to sustain a fund-raising program for the long haul. Very often, particularly in media ministry, an incredible moment will come when, due to TV exposure, a best-selling book, a news story or other convergence of events, the ministry is immediately and dramatically launched into the national spotlight. As a result, the website experiences millions of hits, book sales skyrocket or record donations come in through TV or direct mail.

When that happens, it's wonderful serendipity, and we thank God for it. But if the church or ministry doesn't have a financial plan for the long haul, sooner or later, it's back to oblivion. Time after time I've seen ministries given the remarkable gift of unintended publicity but then drop the ball for a lack of cohesive, long-term financial strategy.

Resource Funding Means Far More than Money

Many churches in this country have amassed an army of volunteers to accomplish remarkable work, an example being the enormous response by churches after Hurricane Katrina in 2005. When the government botched the job early on, it was churches and ministries that stood in the gap and supplied much-needed help and relief. Certainly that response took a significant financial commitment, but what made the real difference was thousands of Christian volunteers helping the recovery efforts.

Facing the Giants

All of this isn't to say that financial partnerships don't work in the nonprofit sector. The African-American church community has been especially innovative in harnessing the power of local businesses to extend their outreach and work. Obviously, caution is in order when churches become landlords and business owners, and we have to go to great lengths to keep our focus on mission; but when it works, it can make a strong statement to the culture.

Pastor Michael Catt of Sherwood Baptist Church in Albany, Georgia, motivated by church media director Alex Kendrick, encouraged his church members to produce, act and market a feature motion picture. *Facing the Giants*, a touching story about a year in the life of a Christian high school football coach and his team, received so much attention that Sony Pictures picked it up for distribution in theaters nationwide. Thanks to the massive volunteer contribution of its members, they were able to produce the picture for a budget of only $100,000, and it made millions at the box office and DVD sales.

That team went on to make other films, like *Fireproof* and *Courageous*—all great box-office successes.

Can a local church impact the entire country?

Absolutely.

Whatever the engine is that drives your funding, without a clear, cohesive brand identity, it will be very tough to instill the kind of motivation in donors, volunteers or partners to make your vision happen.

It's the brand that helps you gain momentum, because it's rarely the one-time spark or brilliant campaign that generates major income, but rather the long-term, steady, day-by-day strategy of forward movement. When your identity conveys an image of confidence, vision, commitment and determination, it's far easier to motivate people to make that vision happen, because, as Collins says, people love winners.

That's because brand identity is all about trust. When your congregation, ministry partners, supporters or audience trust you with their financial resources, funding happens. But it must be conveyed through a clear identity, integrity and solid reputation.

Understand the Difference in Leadership

One thing Jim Collins makes clear is that business leadership is often quite different from nonprofit leadership. He calls it the difference between "executive" and "legislative" leadership. In a business—particularly a privately owned company—the chief executive drives the train. He or she makes the decisions; and at least from an authoritative point of view, those decisions are the bottom line.

But in most nonprofits, particularly in a church or ministry setting, leadership involves building coalitions, assembling teams and practicing bilateral cooperation. This book isn't a treatise on leadership, but it's important to realize the difference. Growing up as a pastor's son in a small church in Charlotte, North Carolina, I watched from the front row as my father had to deal with the elder board, church committees, deacons and other influential members in order to make decisions happen. He became an expert at building coalitions and "working the room."

Today, particularly in independent churches and ministries, I often see more executive-style leadership, and this isn't necessarily a bad thing. In a nonprofit founded by a single person with a clear, unified vision, a board usually exists; but it's often little more than an advisory group, especially when the ministry is built around the testimony or calling of a particular person. Sometimes this happens when the organization begins as a small mom-and-pop ministry and, over a period of years, grows into a national outreach.

There are a couple of different viewpoints on the issue, and this isn't the place for that discussion. I do believe that a visionary leader of a church or ministry shouldn't be held back by an obstinate board or by disgruntled church members. If God has chosen this person for a leadership role, I'll usually default to their decisions. Especially when accountability measures are in place, I'm often comfortable giving them wider latitude in church or ministry leadership.

But I've also seen latitude horribly abused by egotistical leaders who live lives of moral compromise under the auspices of "prophetic vision." They get a bit too used to the power, prestige and financial incentives of national ministry leadership, and they use their position as ruler more than leader. Some, of course, have caused great damage to the faith through moral, financial or leadership abuse.

The key to balance is to understand that in most ministry situations, we can't simply copy leadership from a business perspective. When legislative leadership is required, we need to understand the difference and act accordingly. Granted, many leadership experts will say that part of being true leaders is to understand the difference and respond appropriately; and with that, I would agree.

The Ability to Deliver

An important word on the issue of leadership in the nonprofit sector has to do with your ability to deliver on your promise. Whether you raise money for building water wells in Africa, pregnancy clinics in Cleveland, gang intervention in Los Angeles or evangelism to Eastern Europe, you have to accomplish the mission for your organization to continue.

I've already mentioned that you can't brand a lie. You can't create a brand identity around a specific mission and never show results. People will follow you for a time, but sooner or later they start asking questions. Granted, experience has shown us that the Christian television audience is quite gullible, and millions of dollars have been donated to questionable causes, flawed theology, bad teaching and evangelists with questionable morals (not to mention really bad hair). But over the long haul, building your ministry through results is the key to success.

Creating that mindshare with your support base cannot be overestimated. Jim Collins gives the following example of how the power of a brand is the key to building a great identity:

> Does Harvard truly deliver a better education and do better academic work than other universities? Perhaps, but the emotional pull of Harvard overcomes any doubt when it comes to raising funds. Despite having an endowment in excess of $20 billion, donations continue to flow. As one Harvard graduate put it, "I give money to Harvard every year, and sometimes I feel like I'm bringing sand to the beach." Does the Red Cross truly do the best job of disaster relief? Perhaps, but the brand reputation of the Red Cross gives people an easy answer to the question, "How can I help?" when a disaster hits. Is the American Cancer Society the best mechanism for conquering cancer, or the Nature Conservancy the most effective at protecting the environment? Perhaps, but their brand reputations give people an easy way to support a cause they care about. The same applies to government-funded entities. NYPD has a brand. The United States Marine Corps has a brand. NASA has a brand. Anyone seeking to cut funding must contend with the brand.[3]

Brand Equity

This type of identity leads us to the issue of "brand equity." In this case, the term "equity" isn't about money; it's about the "savings account" you've built with your brand in the minds of your customers.

Once the mindshare with your customer or audience is created, you can begin to deepen the relationship to new levels. Media researcher Erik Du Plessis describes it as "the number of people who will buy the brand with the 'least thinking.'"[4] The customer has no concerns, and very little mental discussion, about the purchase. It's like a "brand memory" built from years of positive feelings about the product, person or institution.

In the religious world, the Billy Graham Evangelistic Association (BGEA) has enormous brand equity when it comes to fulfilling its mission. As a result of years of ministry achievement around the world, millions of lives touched and enormous integrity, BGEA has created extremely positive feelings from its supporters and the general public as well. With that kind of brand equity, an organization can weather very difficult times and still retain a positive relationship with the public.

Brand equity isn't just about overcoming scandal, poor sales or some other disaster. Brand equity makes marketing easier because it's far easier to sell the brand. In other words, you're building on the fact that people already know you, like you and want a relationship with you. In advertising there are two main thrusts: current or past customers and new potential customers. Brand equity helps most with current or past customers, because it helps overcome obstacles or hesitation to repurchase. When they already trust the brand, you don't have to spend the time, money and effort telling customers who you are, what you're about and how you or your product can change their life.

Smashing the Brand

Shortly after the turn of the last century, a designer named Earl R. Dean was working at the Root Glass Company and was given an assignment to design a soft drink bottle that could accomplish two things.

First, it could be recognized in the dark. Simply by touching the bottle, the customer would know the brand of soft drink almost instinctively. Second, even if the bottle was smashed to pieces, the customer could pick up any broken shard and still tell at first glance what the drink had been.

Dean first went for inspiration to the cocoa bean pod, which had contours that were unlike any soft drink bottle on the market. Then, after a great deal of design and development, he unveiled what has become known as the Coca-Cola contourization strategy that used shape to express the brand.

The classic Coke bottle has become one of the most famous icons ever designed and is recognized in virtually every country on the planet. Even today, after plenty of competitors have long since gone out of business, the Coke bottle is still in service, proving the power of the "smash test."

Thousands of companies today use the smash test to evaluate their brands. In other words, if your logo was removed from the product, would the colors, graphics, style or other distinctive images still express the brand? Even better, how much could you smash your organization and still have it reflect your brand? Is your brand so much a part of your organization's DNA that every single aspect of your business reflects the brand?

Branding isn't just a matter of brochures and website designs. It's the story of your organization expressed through customer service, building design, uniforms, procedures and policies, employee training, attitude, and so much more.

Getting Back to the Core

On Saturday, February 24, 2006, the *Wall Street Journal* reported on the contents of a nearly 800-word internal memo written by Starbucks chairman Howard Schultz to his employees. At the time, Starbucks had grown to 13,000 locations, with the goal of establishing 40,000 locations around the globe. Reminding employees that "success is not an entitlement," Schultz was concerned about the growing competition from other fast-food restaurants that had begun going head to head with Starbucks in coffee sales.

But his real focus was the fear of losing the Starbucks story on the global journey toward massive growth. In recent years, the company had begun switching to automatic espresso machines, allowing the coffee to be served faster and eliminating the need to grind beans or pull espresso shots by hand. In their efforts to increase speed and efficiency, Schultz wondered if they had lost much of the romance and theater of the Starbucks coffee experience.

The new automatic machines blocked the sight line, so the customer had lost the ability to interact with the barista to see their beverage being made; and without grinding, they lost the sensory experience of smelling the fresh roasted beans. Mr. Schultz described it as "the loss of aroma—perhaps the most powerful non-verbal signal we had in our stores."

Howard Schultz knows it's about having a great coffee experience and that perhaps in pursuit of modernization and efficiency that core element of the brand was being lost.

What have you lost in the pursuit of expansion and growth? Growth is a wonderful thing, but be very careful what you sacrifice to reach your goals. Brand equity and customer trust are extremely difficult to earn, so be very careful how you grow.

Take Your **Thinking Deeper**

1. What can you do to make everyone in your organization a "brand evangelist"?

2. Your brand isn't just a *strategy*—it's *who you are*. Do you live out your brand every day and with every interaction? Is your story or message coming through loud and clear in every communication, every social media connection, every sale and every opportunity?

3. Are you intentionally encouraging change in your organization? Are you helping people understand the importance of sharing your authentic story?

4. Are there areas or people in your organization that are resistant to change? Identify them and lay out the steps it will take to shift their thinking.

5. Remember that your mission is the most important thing you do. Money is important, and profit matters. However, never allow profit or material success to become the only driver of your organization. How are you keeping your mission in front of your customers, donors, congregation or followers?

6. Can your brand be "smashed" and still be identified as your brand? Is your story and message reflected in every aspect of your organization down to the smallest detail?

The moment you begin to think of yourself as great, your slide toward mediocrity will have already begun.

Jim Collins
Good to Great

In times of change, learners inherit the earth, while the learned find themselves beautifully equipped to deal with a world that no longer exists.

Eric Hoffer
Social Philosopher

The Future of Branding Faith

In 2007, while directing and producing a feature documentary film called *The Better Hour* on the life and work of British Parliamentarian William Wilberforce, I discovered that one of the first and most well-known images of the eighteenth-century abolitionist movement in England was a brand. The focus of the brand was a medallion featuring the image of a kneeling African man.

William Wilberforce had struggled for more than a decade to end the slave trade throughout the British Empire. As a member of Parliament, he had argued, debated, organized and tried everything in his power to change the thinking of the English populace on the issue, but his struggle continued.

Driven by his Christian faith, and supported by his friend John Newton, a former slave trader himself, and writer of the classic hymn "Amazing Grace," he pressed on, trying to make the public aware that they should view slavery as the evil it really was and make an historic change throughout the world.

But the slavery business was the largest industry in the Empire. Some scholars today equate that the financial impact to England of its loss would have been similar to the loss of the defense industry in America today. The forces for continuing the trade were massive and powerful throughout the country.

Growing ever more frustrated, Wilberforce commissioned Josiah Wedgewood, creator of the legendary pottery and china, to design a medallion "expressive of an African in chains in a supplicating posture." The words surrounding the nearly naked man were engraved as a motto: Am I Not A Man And A Brother?

Strategically, the phrase was designed to appeal to both Christians and secularists, and it made an immediate impression on British society. In 1788, an order of the cameos was shipped to Benjamin Franklin in Philadelphia, and wearing the cameo became a fashion statement for abolitionists and antislavery sympathizers in the United States. They were worn as jewelry of all kinds and were mounted like pictures on walls in homes. They also adorned hair combs and snuffboxes.

There is a simple way to package information that, under the right circumstances, can make it irresistible. All you have to do is find it.

Malcolm Gladwell
The Tipping Point[1]

The general public was enthralled, and the image started to appear in major pamphlets of the day. The goal was to focus public opinion on the slave trade, and it worked. Before long, the momentum changed the debate in Parliament, and Wilberforce and his supporters finally won the day.

The medallion had done what years of debate, intellectual discussion and governmental action could not do alone. It helped change the culture and end the slave trade in the British Empire.

When a powerful story and indelible image is connected to a person, cause, product or organization, anything can happen.

Branding Is Not a Religion

At the beginning of this book, we looked at the religious roots of branding, but there is no question that branding is not an end in itself. Since I published the original *Branding Faith,* I've been amazed at the number of branding companies that have popped up specifically to work with churches and religious organizations. Many of these companies are doing excellent work. But I'm also finding that for many, "branding" has become a virtual religion. I got a call from a religious ministry the other day who said, "We've just spent $400,000 on a branding study, have a 250-page branding manual, and have no idea what to do with it."

That's so wrong on so many levels. Branding should be a tool that helps you share your story more effectively. It influences your perception and helps cut through the clutter of multiple messages to tell your story. *What it shouldn't become is a one-size-fits-all solution.* No branding study, brand statement or logo design will overcome bad preaching at a church, poor performance at a nonprofit or a badly written book or screenplay.

Your story is bound up with the unique quality of your content, your DNA and the confidence that comes from acting in your strengths. A great branding study will help you discover your strengths, your identity and your unique story, and it will help you express it well. But if your organization is dysfunctional or if the leadership is failing, spending money to enhance your brand is only putting a new coat of paint on a car with no engine.

Branding Isn't an Exact Science

Branding is organic, reflecting the changing culture, trends and ideas of each generation. Feminists, gender activists, multiculturalists, environmentalists, antiwar protesters, political bloggers, conservatives, liberals, unions, corporations and others understand the power of creating a media identity and using it to engage millions of people every day.

And it works.

While most of these organizations are admired for the ways they've used the media to advance their causes, we in the Christian community are, for the most part, still way behind the curve.

Not so long ago, we thought political power would accomplish our goals, but we realized it could backfire. We tried to shove people around with boycotts but alienated the very people we were trying to reach. We became allied with political causes and parties, and we estranged ourselves from the culture.

The intersection of faith and politics isn't the purpose of this book; but when it comes to branding, I wonder how far political power has really taken us. I definitely encourage Christians to vote, to be politically active and never hesitate to express their faith in the public square. But as we've taken "Christianity" into the political arena, I worry that our cause for Christ has suffered.

There's no question that the Christian faith has been most effective when it has acted as salt and light. Operating on the margins of society, we've made a great contribution to the culture; and as I've said many times, it doesn't take a scholar to note the remarkable and unparalleled contribution Christianity has made to the West throughout history.

But in what most call a postmodern and post-Christian culture, we're discovering that any power we thought we had has created a backlash. Even though they acted with the best of intentions, Christian leaders of a generation ago who made Christianity a political force are now viewed by the culture as parodies and are often referred to in condescending and humorous terms.

I'm not here to argue their accomplishments, but I am here to offer a better way to impact the culture for the future.

Reaching the next generation isn't about political power; it's about branding power. It's not about what we're against; it's about what we're for. It's not about changing the culture from the outside; it's about changing the culture from the inside.

Branding is about creating a compelling story of what the Christian faith is, what it stands for and how it can change lives. Ultimately, it's about *meaning*.

The search for meaning is the most powerful force in the world. It's more powerful than politics, big business and even war. As this country becomes more and more polarized politically, the only thing that will break through that bleak wall of separation is *meaning*. When we can show the culture that we're not against them, that we have a compelling story and that the story can change their circumstances, I believe they will listen.

The book *The Da Vinci Code*, written primarily as a suspenseful detective story, made outrageous claims about the origins of the Christian faith that had little or nothing to do with the actual truth. And yet, the culture bought into the story to such an extent that the book became one of the biggest sellers of all time, and the movie version experienced major box office results as well.

For many leaders in the religious community, it was the apocalypse. To see the public race in such numbers to bookstores and movie theaters to view such an obviously defective story was certainly depressing, and many reacted with understandable indignation.

But the fact is, there will always be plenty of other books and movies that scorn our religious values and offend our faith. So how should we react? Should we use our political and marketing power to boycott, protest and complain, or should we somehow engage these often-offensive entertainment projects?

Looking back at movies and TV programs, from *The Da Vinci Code* to ABC's (now canceled) *Good Christian Bitches* (actually released as *GCB* as a response to criticism), I've been thinking about the reaction of the Christian community and what we can learn in retrospect. I've been interviewed on plenty of national media outlets, and I often discuss the fact that Christianity seems to be the last subject people can criticize without fear of reprisal. Can you imagine if a major studio released a movie that said Muhammad and Islam were frauds? Or a network TV program called *Good Muslim Bitches*?

The public would be outraged.

A few years ago, on a national comedy network, the producers of an edgy and controversial animated cartoon series put the network to the test and filmed scenes that disparaged both Mohammed and Jesus. And just as the producers probably expected, the network refused to show Mohammed being made fun of, and censored the scene. But with Jesus, the ridicule was just fine.

What should we learn?

Boycotts are the "nuclear option" only, and must be used carefully. A number of years ago here in Los Angeles, there was a massive nationwide boycott by the Mexican community over the issue of illegal immigration. In spite of a huge turnout, the leaders of that movement immediately began to question its success. Many worried that it created bad feelings with the public and may have done more harm than good in spite of hundreds of thousands of people that turned out across the country, and massive media coverage.

During one boycott of a major film studio by one of America's largest Christian denominations, the studio's sales actually went up. So we need to be careful with boycotts and use them only when absolutely necessary and with great strategic planning.

Start the conversation with the culture. It's interesting that after my appearances on most of the talk shows, non-Christian producers and staff would come up and introduce themselves, congratulate me and say things like, "Wow, I didn't know there were Christians out there who thought this way." They wanted to talk with someone about the movie but were afraid of most of the Christians who loudly disapproved of the film. We must put down our protest signs, stop bullying, reach out our hands and begin the dialogue.

Use the available resources. As *The Da Vinci Code* film was released, I was very excited about all the seminars, books, teaching materials and other resources marshaled to point people to the real truth of the Bible. Websites pointed thousands of people to some of our most brilliant scholars and leaders who provided important information to help as they shared their faith with friends and family. Even the *Los Angeles Times* reported on the incredible number of pastors who used the film as a teaching tool to share the correct information about Christianity.

Don't get distracted from your original assignment. Too many Christians get so caught up in controversial issues that they lose their focus on reaching the world with a message of hope. Yes, politics, culture, poverty, social problems, media and a host of other issues are vitally important, but we need to keep them in the perspective of the Great Commission. Don't get distracted from your original calling.

One movie or TV show isn't going to bring down the faith that transformed the world. As I said in some of my interviews, this movie won't create a nation of agnostics or atheists. Yes, some will be duped; but frankly, the Christian faith defeated the Roman Empire and transformed music, literature, the arts, scholarship and science throughout Europe and the West. Although I'm always ready to share my faith, and I'm concerned about the moral decay of the culture, I'm not too worried that God really needs defending. He's done pretty well since the creation of the world. I think He'd rather have me spend more time focusing on loving my neighbor.

Individual believers need to be active in politics, from our local communities to the national level. But we must be very careful not to use our perceived political clout as a club. A far better way is to engage the culture; and the most hopeful method is through telling a powerful brand story.

Our ultimate goal is to win their hearts, and that only comes from the inside.

Your brand will grow and succeed only if it deserves it. If your brand is connecting to the audience, giving their lives meaning and helping them accomplish their goals in life, then it will continue to sustain its impact.

I close this book with a quote from, of all people, Charles Darwin, the man whose theory of evolution has caused so much chaos, conflict and concern during the last century. I'm not a scientist, but I do know that whatever you think of his theories, Darwin got at least one thing right. He said:

It is not the strongest of the species that survive, nor the most intelligent, but rather the one most responsive to change.

Change happens, and change is coming whether we like it or not; whether we bemoan modern advertising and marketing, criticize those who are pioneering new ideas or turn our backs on new technology. Jesus criticized the Pharisees for not recognizing the signs of the times, and yet 2,000 years later, leaders of churches, ministries and nonprofits are still just as blind.

Creating an effective brand story doesn't mean being *reactive* to the culture; it means being *responsive* to the culture—recognizing the change and being there with the story that has transformed so many generations before us.

Don't give your congregation, your donors or your audience what you think they want.

Give them what they never dreamed possible.

Take Your **Thinking Deeper**

1. Branding is vitally important in today's media-driven culture. But ultimately, it's not about branding; it's

about telling your story. Branding is a tool, not a religion. Never let more and more branding surveys, workshops or evaluations get in the way of telling your story well.

2. Now go for it!

Prologue: Responding to a Media-driven Culture
1. James B. Twitchell, *Branded Nation* (New York: Simon and Schuster, 2005).

Introduction: Losing Our Voice
1. James B. Twitchell, *Branded Nation* (New York: Simon and Schuster, 2005), p. 47.
2. Ibid., p. 59.
3. Douglas B. Sosnick, Matthew J. Dowd and Ron Fournier, *Appplebee's America: How Successful Political, Business, and Religious Leaders Connect with the New American Community* (New York: Simon and Schuster, 2006), p. 2.

Chapter 1: Living in a Media-driven Culture
1. Michael J. Wolf, *The Entertainment Economy: How Mega-Media Forces Are Transforming Our Lives* (New York: Times Books, 1999), p. 4.
2. Marty Neumeier, *The Brand Gap* (Berkeley, CA: Peachpit Press, 2005), p. 40.
3. BLS American Time Use Survey, A.C. Nielsen Co. (2-7-2012).
4. Denise Gellene, "Teens Who Use Cell Phones Most Found to Be Sadder and Less Assured," *Los Angeles Times,* May 24, 2006 (reporting on a meeting of the American Psychiatric Association in Toronto).
5. James B. Twitchell, *Branded Nation* (New York: Simon & Schuster Paperbacks, 2005), p. 2.

Chapter 4: A New Religion?
1. Wally Olins, *Wally Olins. On Br@nd* (New York: Thames and Hudson, 2003), p. 11.
2. Tom Boudoin, *Consuming Faith: Integrating Who We Are with What We Buy* (Lanham, MD: Sheed and Ward, 2003), p. xiii.
3. Patrick Hanlon, *Primal Branding* (New York: Free Press, 2006), pp. 9-85.
4. Ibid., p. 70.
5. Sonny Arguinzoni, Jr., cited in Sarah Eekhoff Zylstra, "City Shuts Down Church Club," *Christianity Today*, March 2012, p. 12.
6. Linda Tischler, "How Do I Love Thee? Let Me Plot the Graph," *Fast Company*, July 2004, no. 84, p. 64.
7. Martin Lindstrom, "Religion: Inspiration for Brands," The Branding Strategy Insider, May 4, 2007. http://www.brandingstrategyinsider.com/2007/05/religion_inspir.html#more (accessed November 2007).
8. Ibid.

Chapter 5: Telling Your Story
1. Peter Montoya with Tim Vandehey, *The Brand Called You* (Tustin, CA: Personal Branding Press, 2003), pp. 42-43,53.
2. Ibid., p. 41.
3. America Online Poll, November 9, 2006.

Chapter 6: The Right Branding Tools
1. Douglas B. Sosnick, Matthew J. Dowd and Ron Fournier, *Applebee's America: How Successful Political, Business and Religious Leaders Connect with the New American Community* (New York: Simon and Schuster, 2006), p. 65.

2. Neil Postman, *Amusing Ourselves to Death* (New York: Penguin Books, 1985), p. 7.

3. Malcolm Muggeridge, *Christ and the Media* (Grand Rapids, MI: William B. Eerdmans Publishing Co., 1977), p. 64.

4. Ibid., p. 106.

5. Ibid., p. 58.

6. Sosnick, Dowd and Fournier, *Applebee's America: How Successful Political, Business and Religious Leaders Connect with the New American Community,* p. 69.

Chapter 7: Why Social Media Matters

1. Mark Dreistadt, "The Four Revolutions." According to Dreistadt, "Delphi offered first a national commercial online email connection (July 1992) and soon after a full Internet service (November 1992)."

2. "Demographics of Internet Users," Pew Internet & American Life Project, 2012 data. http://pewinternet.org/Static-Pages/Trend-Data-%28Adults%29/Whos-Online.aspx

3. Emil Protalinski, "Facebook Has Over 845 Million Users," ZDNet. http://www.zdnet.com/blog/facebook/facebook-has-over-845-million-users/8332.

4. Rosa Golijan, "Twitter's 140 Million Users Tweet Over 400 Million Times Per Day," Technology, NBCNews.com. http://www.technolog.msnbc.msn.com/technology/technolog/twitters-140-million-users-tweet-over-400-million-times-day-817887.

5. "WordPress Sites in the World," WordPress.com. http://en.wordpress.com/stats/.

6. "Tumblr: About Us." http://www.tumblr.com/about.

7. Mike Tuttle, "Social Media Networks Reach 1.2 Billion Users Worldwide," WebPro news, January 6, 2012. http://www.webpronews.com/social-networks-reach-1-2-billion-users-worldwide-2012-01.

8. The three values come from David Allen, writing for *Business Week.*

9. Leonard Sweet, *Viral: How Social Networking Is Poised to Ignite Revival* (Colorado Springs, CO: Waterbrook Press, 2012), p. 50.

10. David Westerman, Patric R. Spence, Brandon Van Der Heide, "A Social Network as Information: The Effect of System Generated Reports of Connectedness on Credibility on Twitter," *Computers in Human Behavior,* January 2012, vol. 28, no 1, pp. 199-206.

Chapter 8: Great Design

1. Virginia Postral, *The Substance of Style: How the Rise of Aesthetic Value Is Remaking Commerce, Culture, and Consciousness* (New York: Harper Perennial, 2004), p. 2.

2. D. K. Holland, *Branding for Non-Profits: Developing Identity with Integrity* (New York: Allworth Press, 2006), p. 71.

Chapter 9: The Dark Side of Branding

1. Mercer Schuchardt, "Swooshtika: Icons for Corporate Tribes," September 13, 2002. http://www.theooze.com/articles/article.cfm?id=132 (accessed November 2006).

2. http://mashable.com/2010/10/14/nielsen-texting-stats/.

3. Ely Portillo, "Loneliness Looks Popular These Days," Knight Ridder News Service, June 23, 2006. http://www.signonsandiego.com/uniontrib/20060623/news_1n23lonely.html (accessed November 2007).

4. Ibid.

5. Shane Hipps, *The Hidden Power of Electronic Culture* (Grand Rapids, MI: Zondervan, 2005), p. 112.

6. Janet Kornblum, "Meet My 5,000 New Best Pals," *USA Today*, September 19, 2006. http://www.usatoday.com/tech/news/2006-09-19-friending_x.htm (accessed November 2007).

7. Neil Postman, *Amusing Ourselves to Death* (New York: Penguin Books, 1985), pp. vii-viii.

8. Erwin McManus, speech to National Religious Broadcasters Conference (February 18, 2007), Orlando, FL.

9. Robyn Waters, *The Trendmaster's Guide: Get a Jump on What Your Customer Wants Next* (New York: Penguin Group, 2005), p. xi.

10. Ibid.

11. Os Guinness, *Prophetic Untimeliness* (Grand Rapids, MI: Baker Books, 2005), p. 65.

12. Philip D. Kenneson and James L. Street, *Selling Out the Church* (Nashville, TN: Abingdon Press, 1997), p. 143.

13. Philip D. Kenneson and James L. Street, Selling Out the Church (Eugene, OR: Wipf and Stock Publishers, 1997), p. 80.

14. Robert F. Lusch, "Marketing's Evolving Identity: Defining Our Future," American Marketing Association. http://www.marketingpower.com/content2018879.php (accessed November 2007).

15. Walter Brueggemann, *Biblical Perspectives on Evangelism: Living in a Three-Storied Universe* (Nashville, TN: Abingdon Press, 1993), p. 88.

Chapter 10: The Branding Imperative

1. Wally Olins, *Wally Olins. On Brand* (New York: Thames and Hudson, 2004), p. 89.

2. Jim Collins, *Good to Great in the Social Sectors* (Boulder, CO: Jim Collins, 2005), p. 2.

3. Ibid., p. 25.

4. Erik Du Plessis, *The Advertised Mind* (Sterling, VA: Millward Brown and Kogan Page Limited, 2005), p. 197.

Chapter 11: The Future of Branding Faith

1. Malcolm Gladwell, *The Tippping Point* (New York: Back Bay Books, 2002), p. 132.

Unique